THE QUEEN OF GRANTS 2

GrantTalk Secrets for the New Era of Grant Writing

LIBBY HIKIND

Edition Information

First hardcover edition
ISBN: 979-8-9921123-5-1

First paperback edition
ISBN: 978-1-967592-26-5

First eBook edition
ISBN: 978-1-967592-28-9

Publisher

Libby Hikind Books LLC
Published under the GrantWatch imprint

6400 Boynton Beach Blvd., Suite 742911
Boynton Beach, FL 33437
United States

www.libbyhikind.com

Printed in the United States of America.

Dedication

This book is dedicated to my beloved children, grandchildren, and great-grandchildren.

My message to them and to all my readers:

The future is not predicted; it is created.

Fear is natural,

but confidence grows through action.

Each step forward

creates what comes next.

As you move, your eyes open to possibilities.

Act with intention.

Stay flexible.

Libby Hikind

Also, By Libby Hikind

Business, Grants & Personal Development

- *The Queen of Grants: From Teacher to Grant Writer to CEO*
- *The Queen of Grants 2: GrantTalk Secrets for the New Era of Grant Writing*
- *Organizing My Thoughts, Manifesting My Goals 2026: A Journal for Reflection, Planning, and Achievement*

Children's Picture Books & Stories

- *Bailey Bullied Me: And I Am Kinder Now*
- *Fifty Stars Go Back to School: The Cheat Sheet That Became the Study Guide*
- *Mr. Squirrel's Spring Cleaning Lesson: A Tale of Tidiness and Teamwork*
- *Rikki Wants a Pet: How a Fluttery Surprise Saved the Day*
- *Twig Literacy: A Fun Story About Beavers, Money (Twigs), and Saving*
- *Why Won't You Fly, Sky?: A Tale of Finding the Courage to Soar*
- *Why Won't You Go to School, Kiki Kangaroo?: How Everyone Helped Him, School Is Scary Until It's Not*
- *Ziva the Zebra Runs Away: A Story About the Beauty of Being Yourself*

Activity, Coloring & Companion Books

- *Bailey Bullied Me Activity Marker Coloring Book*
- *Fifty Stars Go Back to School: Color the Story*
- *Kiki Kangaroo Activity Coloring Book*
- *Kiki Kangaroo Activity Marker Coloring Book*
- *Mr. Squirrel's Spring Cleaning Lesson Activity & Coloring Book*
- *Twig Literacy Activity Coloring Book*
- *Twig Literacy Activity Marker Coloring Book*
- *Why Won't You Fly, Sky? Activity & Coloring Book*
- *Why Won't You Go to School, Kiki Kangaroo? Activity Coloring Book*
- *Ziva the Zebra Runs Away: Color the Story*

All books can be found on *LibbyHikind.com*

TABLE OF CONTENTS

TESTIMONIALS

"Libby Hikind has done it again. The Queen of Grants 2 is packed with real-world strategies and insights straight from funders and grant recipients, making it one of the most practical grant resources available today. If you want to win more grants and build long-term funding relationships, this book is a must-read." *_Jason R. Hill, Founder of 'OWWLL' and Host of 'The Shrimp Tank'*

"This book is for anyone interested in grant writing, including executive directors, board members, staff, and volunteers. The information Libby provides is essential for understanding what grantors are looking for and for building relationships to secure continued funding. It is a comprehensive toolkit that will help nonprofits effectively utilize grants to fund their missions.*"_Melanie Reeves, Executive Director at RiverLife*

"The Queen of Grants 2 is a must-read for nonprofits looking for practical advice on how to get started in grant writing. Libby's ability to share the intricacies of effective grant writing has enabled our organization to secure many grants. GrantWatch continues to be our go-to resource when seeking grant opportunities." *_Bobbi Donovan, President and CEO, Sunshine Family Outreach Center*

"What sets Libby Hikind apart is the combination of deep expertise and insatiable curiosity, ensuring that The Queen of Grants 2 reflects the most up-to-date and relevant landscape in the field. She is, without question, a wonderful authority on the subject. The Queen of Grants 2 feels like a conversation with the mentor you wished you had." *_Alexis Hyde, Executive Director of the Quinn Emanuel Arts Foundation*

"By sharing insights from the people who are making funding decisions, Libby's new book gives grant writers an all-access pass to new considerations and processes in the field." *_Sarah Lyding, Executive Director, The Music Man Foundation*

"Grant writing can be overwhelming if you haven't written one before. As more grants become available for small businesses, more training is needed to help secure funds. This book will help both novice and more experienced grant writers to: research. prepare and submit grants." *_Nan Devlin, Consultant and Grant Manager, Rural Tourism Partners, (former Executive Director of Tillamook Coast Visitors Association)*

"I really appreciated my conversation with Libby! It gave me the opportunity to connect with her audience, share some insight into why we ask the questions we do, and explain how to prepare before submitting a grant application. It's wonderful that this information is being included in her upcoming book, and I'm glad to be a part of it." *_Laurel Meleski, Director of Operations at RedRover*

"The Queen of Grants 2 brings together expertise from many sectors to show steps for grant success and pitfalls to avoid, whether you seek funding for arts, healthcare, or social services. I highly recommend this book to anyone who is new to grant writing or who wants to refresh best practices." *_Brenda Swann, Director of Grants and Operations at St. Johns Cultural Council*

"I love the spirit of collaboration that Libby brings to nonprofits. She encourages a deeper dive into sharing resources and provides tips and insights to help us improve our chances of securing funding. Wishing you the best in your book launch!" *_Lisa-Marie Haygood, Executive Director of the Cherokee County Educational Foundation*

"Being featured in The Queen of Grants 2 is an honor. Our music program grew through thoughtful, multi-year funding and strong community partnerships, and this book reflects that same strategic approach. It's a practical and inspiring guide for organizations seeking to use grants as a catalyst for meaningful, sustainable impact. I plan to make it a primary reference as I continue to pursue grant funding in the future." *_Raquel "Kell" Chole, Founder and Executive Director of the Institute of Traditional Irish Music and Murphy Roche School of Irish Music*

"Libby Hikind's GrantWatch has been my top tool for searching grants. The insights she and grants professionals share are practical, to the point, and extremely helpful." _*Karen Harvey, Grant Writer at Westminster at Wade (DBA Wade Center)*

"We are grateful for the opportunity to share our story with Libby Hikind and appreciate her fine work in spreading information about our grant program. We received numerous requests from both individuals and nonprofit organizations following our appearance on the podcast. Ms. Hikind is very knowledgeable about both grant writing and accessing grants. I am confident this book will be helpful to those seeking guidance on securing a grant." _*Sharon McGraw, Ed.D., Grant Program Officer at Community Fund Ohio*

"It is such a great honor to have this opportunity to be a part of this wonderful book. We have been members of the GrantWatch program since 2023; words cannot express our appreciation for a program we can rely on, where we can research grants at our leisure. We all know that grants can be very difficult and demanding. Because of this great program, we are able to seek out the information needed to complete our grant application in a timely manner. If you are not a member of this wonderful program, I highly recommend joining. You will find that this program is very beneficial to you and your organization. Thank you so much for giving me this opportunity."_*George Vaughn, Founder and President of StreeHeat Ministries, a Nonprofit Charitable Corporation in North Las Vegas*

"Grant Watch is a valuable tool to be able to share best practices from people working day-in and day-out to improve their communities at the local level. Grant writing can be daunting, but it's a skill anyone willing to try can learn! Learning from others who have done it successfully will help you become skilled at it quicker, and this is a really important resource to make that skill sharing possible." *_Ryanne Jennings, President and CEO of the Wayne County Community Foundation*

"I sincerely recommend The Queen of Grants 2 by Libby Hikind to every nonprofit client I work with. So many organizations are doing vital, life-changing work in our communities, yet they constantly struggle to find the grant funding necessary to sustain and expand their missions. Libby's book provides a clear blueprint for identifying, pursuing, and securing grant opportunities with confidence and strategy.

When I began working with Libby to promote GrantWatch.com, I was immediately impressed by her determination and vision. From writing The Queen of Grants 1 and now The Queen of Grants 2, to launching a podcast and building the largest grant database in the world through GrantWatch.com, Libby has consistently followed through on her dream with focus and excellence.

Her expertise is not theoretical. It is built on real experience, data, and results. She has created tools that empower nonprofits, municipalities, businesses, and individuals to access funding opportunities that might otherwise remain hidden.

I am incredibly proud to be quoted in this book and honored that our team has played a role in helping put the spotlight on the Queen of Grants.

Congratulations, Libby and Jacob, on this continued success and for equipping so many organizations with the resources they need to thrive."_*Sandy Collier, President of Hey, Sandy! PR & Communications*

"I have been a member of GrantWatch for decades and truly could not imagine working without it!!! The daily grant listings and informative podcasts are invaluable resources for staying current and competitive in grant development. The platform is continually updated and designed for ease of use, making it efficient and reliable.

Whenever questions arise, the GrantWatch team is readily accessible by email or phone and consistently provides prompt, knowledgeable support.

For anyone new to the world of grants and grant writers challenged with seeking diverse funding streams, GrantWatch is an absolute necessity. The online platform serves nonprofits—large and small—in every state, while also supporting individuals and businesses seeking funding opportunities to advance their initiatives and better serve their clients. The daily listings identify and detail federal, state, and foundation grants, clearly outlining funding priorities, award amounts, and application timelines.

Try it, I am confident you will agree that GrantWatch is one of the most comprehensive and dependable grant resources available."
_Helena Kosoff, Grant Writer at Grant Writing by Helena

"But God Ministries appreciates the ease of finding grants and connecting with funders using GrantWatch's software. It is an affordable tool that pays for itself with just one successful grant. This software has helped take BGM from an organization that had never received a grant in 2018 to one that has now received over $4,000,000 in grants." *_Dina Ray, Director of Development for But God Ministries.*

"How does a 60-member band with a $30k budget raise $1.4 million for a new home? For the Sequim City Band, the answer was WA GrantWatch, which proved instrumental in securing nearly all the funding for their rehearsal hall expansion. After years of playing in cramped quarters, the band has finally traded their tight spaces for a million-dollar upgrade!" *_Dave Proebstel, Former Treasurer (24 years) of the Sequim City Band*

"The Queen of Grants 2 offers a structured, behind-the-scenes look at how funding decisions are actually made. Libby brings together practical insights from operators, funders, and advisors, helping readers think more strategically about growth and sustainability. It is a strong guide for organizations serious about improving their grant outcomes." *_Matt Berkowitz, Founder, AllSet PEO Consultants*

"The Queen of Grants 2 is a masterclass in turning vision into funded reality. As a cybersecurity expert who partners closely with nonprofits, I know how critical a strong funding strategy is, and this book delivers it with clarity and authority. Being featured in its pages was an honor, but what stands out most is how powerfully it equips leaders to think bigger and act smarter. If you are serious about impact, this is your blueprint." *_Elliot Rosenfeld, President and CEO, Net is Up*

INTRODUCTION

Following the success of *The Queen of Grants: From Teacher to Grant Writer to CEO*, this book builds on that foundation, drawing from decades of experience and more than fifty GrantTalk interviews with funders, grantees, and nonprofit leaders.

Thank you for being a *Queen of Grants* reader and for returning to read my second book in the series. I hope you make a positive change in the world.

> ➤ The key themes of this book are represented by the hearts on the cover:
>
> 💜 52 GrantTalk Interviews
>
> 💜 Advice from Funders
>
> 💜 Insights from Grantees
>
> 💜 The 20-Day Platform Challenge
>
> 💜 Grant Eligibility Essentials
>
> 💜 AI-Powered Grant & Funder Search
>
> 💜 AI-Assisted Grant Writing
>
> 💜 Setting Up a Podcast
>
> 💜 Marketing & Growth Strategies

The Queen of Grants 2: GrantTalk Secrets for the New Era of Grant Writing is written for professionals who want to refine their skills, expand their reach, and create new opportunities. It is designed for grant writers, nonprofit professionals, entrepreneurs, and emerging leaders who want to increase both their impact and their income.

Are you ready for what comes next in grant funding? Do you want to elevate your writing, expand your career, and embrace new opportunities? If so, *The Queen of Grants 2* is for you.

Your next chapter begins here. Are you ready to write it?

The Queen of Grants 2: GrantTalk Secrets for the New Era of Grant Writing will give you practical insights into today's grant landscape and will demonstrate how to leverage grant writing skills to expand opportunities, visibility, and revenue.

The book is divided into four key chapters, each of which can be read independently or altogether in its entirety.

I.   GrantTalk Secrets

Brings together insights from 52 *GrantTalk* Episodes of funders, grantees, nonprofit leaders, and subject-matter experts across the United States and Canada. Readers learn how decisions are made, what captures attention, and why strong proposals will rise above the rest. Program development, project design, needs statements, budgeting, evaluation, communication with funders, and the full grant lifecycle are discussed, providing you with a comprehensive foundation for writing grants with clarity, confidence, and purpose.

Podcast guests' titles and organizations are listed throughout and at the conclusion of the chapter, and for the most part, reflect those held at the time of their *GrantTalk* interview.

II.   Marketing and Visibility

Written to help organizations increase recognition, communicate their mission, and stand out in a crowded funding environment, you are guided through branding, social media strategy, content creation, blogging, trending topics, and podcasting.

III.   The 20-Day Platform Challenge

You do not often get to see behind the curtain of a company, and yet, here, for the sake of education and training, the curtain is drawn for a refreshingly honest, behind-the-scenes look at a cross-section of the marketing, development, and customer support team at GrantWatch as they complete a full website refresh on a very tight timeline. Through daily journals and reflections, readers see how ideas take shape, how obstacles are overcome, and how collaboration strengthens progress.

The staff's 20-Day journaling is very relatable, and you will grow to know and love the people who volunteered to participate in the challenge. This model in action demonstrates teamwork, problem-solving, and organizational readiness.

IV.   AI in Grant Writing

New AI proprietary tools developed for GrantWatch subscribers are introduced, and you will be shown how artificial intelligence can sharpen needs, data, research and support early proposal drafting. This chapter will discuss a thoughtful approach to using AI responsibly, while recognizing that human judgment and compelling storytelling remain at the core of every successful proposal. Readers will gain insight into how the foundation directory and grant recipient search were built from public data and Form 990 reports specifically for grant seekers, offering faster access to essential information and saving hours of research time.

With all this in mind, let's begin to dive into the heart of what *GrantTalk* guests have shared, starting with the secrets that can transform your grant journey.

I: GrantTalk Secrets

Whether you are new to grants or looking to sharpen your skills, this chapter walks you through every stage of the process.

GrantTalk Secrets is grounded in real-world insights from people who have written, won, and lost grants, and tried again. The power of this book is in the voices of funders. It is practical advice from professionals who know what works, what fails, and why.

I built this chapter from the first 52 *GrantTalk* interviews with grant funders, grant recipients, and nonprofit professionals who shared their experiences openly and honestly. I asked the questions you would ask. I pressed for clarity. I wanted real answers, not polished sound bites.

I interviewed grant recipients who found grants on GrantWatch, applied, and were awarded. I spoke with leaders and representatives of funding organizations whose grants are listed on GrantWatch. I also interviewed professionals who support nonprofits behind the scenes, including a PR professional, a PEO health insurance consultant, a cybersecurity strategist, and the creator of the OWWLL app.

Then I went deeper. I reviewed transcripts to understand exactly how funders evaluate applications, what makes a proposal stand out, why applications are rejected, and how organizations build lasting funding relationships. The funders featured here are listed on GrantWatch.com, and I encourage you to explore their grants.

Everything in this chapter is cross-referenced with episodes available on GrantWatch on the GrantTalk tab and on the GrantWatch YouTube channel.

At the end of this chapter, you will find a table listing all episodes featured in this series so you can continue learning from the voices that resonate most with your mission. You can also watch the full interviews on the GrantWatch YouTube channel for complete conversations and behind-the-scenes footage.

Now, with their voices in mind, let us address the myths that keep people from even beginning. These are myths I hear repeated in nearly every interview.

Myths Grant Writers Need to Stop Believing

Let's clear something up: You don't need to be a professional writer to apply for a grant. Patty Eljaiek, Long Island Grants for the Arts

Coordinator for Huntington Arts Council (Episode 49), said, "We don't ask you to write a dissertation....We just want you to answer the questions.... There is a word count. Use the words in the question in your answer."

You don't need to have an English degree. You don't even need to have staff.

What do you need? An innovative idea, a real plan, and the willingness and passion to try.

Too many people believe they're "not ready." But guess what? Katy Sursa, Director of Development at United Cerebral Palsy of Arkansas, wasn't ready to apply until she did (Episode 6). Rosaline Bangura, Founder of Be Rose International Foundation (Episode 3), taught herself mid-crisis.

And I, Libby Hikind, was a teacher with an idea and a brand-new Commodore 64 computer (in a sealed box) in the 1980s when I started writing my first grant.

The biggest myth? Grants are only for someone else. They're for you if you're willing to get organized and apply.

These myths often keep people from even starting, but as I discovered while recording *GrantTalk*, funding is far more accessible. Let me share a bit about how these conversations came to life.

The *GrantTalk* Podcast: Behind the Insights

Since publishing *The Queen of Grants: From Teacher to Grant Writer to CEO*, I launched the *"GrantTalk"* podcast. To date, I have personally interviewed 59 guests, comprised of grant funders, recipients, and B2B professionals. Even with my strong background in the grant world, I have been amazed at every interview, as new insights or advice have emerged from grant funders and recipients.

This book encapsulates what we learned from the first 52 episodes of *GrantTalk*. Hosting the *GrantTalk* podcast gave me a front-row seat to how real people, founders and funders, grant writers and board members, navigate the world of grant funding. These conversations brought lessons I couldn't have captured in a guidebook alone.

My interviews covered a wide variety of grants across the USA and Canada, including those in science, education, the arts, business, research, the environment, trails, and more.

I also learned firsthand how current executive directors, grant writers, and nonprofit leaders built their careers.

The interviews from number 53 onward will be integrated into my next book. I had to stop somewhere, and I wanted to publish what I call *Queen 2,* as I call it among my friends and family, within two years of the first book. I apologize to the seven guests who did not make the cut-off for this book: Episodes 53-59. Hopefully, you will be in good company with my future podcast interviewees.

With my premise, that the best time to write your second book (or second grant) is right after the first, I can tell you that I have already started writing *The Queen of Grants 3.*

It's Not About Money, It's About the Mission

Across all these interviews, one theme stood out above the rest: It's not about the money, it's about the mission. As my guests shared, one thing I heard repeatedly was that grants are tools, not goals. Your mission comes first. If your mission is strong and clear, the funding will follow.

Melanie Reeves, Executive Director of RiverLife (Episode 47), shared that a grant her organization discovered on GrantWatch.com helped to fund the installation of 5 wheelchair ramps, directly advancing her mission to serve her community.

One ramp was installed for an 83-year-old wheelchair-bound woman with dementia, who could not leave her house. The woman's daughter told her that, for the first time in a long time, her mother had been able to leave the house and go to church.

A representative from But God Ministries (Episode 4), Dina Ray, Director of Development, discussed her desire to build an entire community in Mississippi, block by block, where water, housing, clinics, and education are all tied to a single purpose of building sustainable communities around the world.

In Episode 44, Homer Bizzle, III put it perfectly: "Our mission is to help veterans become self-[sufficient]. Not giving them a handout, but a hand up."

Advice from Grant Recipients

You'd be surprised how many grant writers started by accident. I can't tell you how often I've heard, "I never meant to become a grant writer, I just saw a need."

Rosaline Bangura (Episode 3) started writing grants during an Ebola crisis; she had no background, just a mission and a reason to act.

Katy Sursa (Episode 6) took on a massive Department of Transportation grant without ever writing one before. All because her organization needed transportation.

This mission-driven mindset shines through in the stories of grant recipients I spoke with, many of whom started just like you or me, without formal training.

And me? I was a special education teacher who just wanted to bring word processors into the classroom to teach my students written communication skills to pass a statewide exam. That first grant changed everything. The lesson here is: if you care enough, you can learn the rest.

Build Your Program First

Building on these accidental successes, a key piece of advice from grant recipients is to focus on your organization before chasing funds.

Don't build your program around a grant. Build your program first, then find a grant that matches. Melanie Reeves, Executive Director of RiverLife (Episode 47), explained that when they received funding, "we already had a list of needs," which allowed her team to organize volunteers immediately and complete the work.

Traci Lanier, Vice President of Institutional Advancement at 10,000 Degrees (Episode 21), shared that her team had already built a strong college access and success program long before applying for major grants. When they expanded into new regions, their proven model helped funders trust them, even without local connections.

Foundations of Grant Writing

Let's cover the foundations of grant writing. I'll break it down step by step, drawing from what funders and recipients shared.

Before your team starts writing a grant, take a step back and ask yourself: Why are we doing this? Not just "we need money", but what's the deeper need in your community that you're trying to meet?

Understanding the Grant Process

To build that strong base, first grasp how grants work; not all processes are created equal.

Eloiza Altoro, Fund Advisor at the Nonprofit Management Fund (Episode 48) said, "It's a pretty simple application, because we don't want organizations to have to jump through a lot of hoops."

Katie Reusch, Director of Youth Programs at YSA (Youth Service America) [at the time of filming] (Episode 20), explained that their youth-led service grants are intentionally simple. The application process is short and accessible, but still structured around impact, volunteer engagement, and measurable goals.

As Magda Galindo, Director of Grants Management at FFAR, explained in Episode 41, they fund research in a few main ways, and the process changes based on how you apply. "We fund our research... in four major ways. We have our direct solicitations and our competitive request for applications, or RFAs. We also do prizes and competitions, and we do consortia... public-private stakeholders that come together to fund projects in an area that everyone is interested in."

Magda continued, "So, our application process can vary... because it depends on which of those mechanisms you come through... Some of our applications... are considered a two-stage process... You go through a letter of intent (LOI) step... usually just a one-pager where you tell us what kind of research you're interested in pursuing and whether it meets our needs... If it does, you're then invited to submit a full proposal, and that's what... carries the meat and potatoes of the research..."

Another foundation (Episode 29) described a more formal two-step review process: a two-page pre-proposal first, followed by a full application for those invited to continue. Each proposal is reviewed for mission fit, methodology, and budget alignment.

These are good examples and explanations of why it may be a good idea to start with something short, such as an LOI, to see if your idea fits before diving in.

Rolling Applications Do Not Always Mean First Come, First Funded

During COVID, funds were used up quickly as they were funded on a first-come, first-served basis. In Florida, grants for a new roof are also funded that way.

It would therefore be natural to assume that if a funder accepts applications on a rolling basis, submitting early increases their chances; that is not always the case. If there is someone to ask, ask before rushing.

Some funders accept applications on a rolling basis but wait to review all applications until after the deadline. They do not favor early submissions.

In other words, rolling submission can be about flexibility for applicants, not speed as a competitive advantage. With timing in mind, let's turn to the core of what makes a grant application stand out. What is a thoughtful program design that truly engages your community?

Program Design and Volunteer Engagement

Cutting costs in your organizational budget, in your program, or as a component of your overall budget comes down to networking for better solutions and to including reliable volunteerism.

Designing a strong program means knowing how to engage your team and your volunteers.

Jason Hill, Founder and Creator of the OWWLL app and host of Shrimp Tank (Episode 28), discussed how nonprofits can use his platform to find subject-matter experts and board members. It's not just about the program, it's about who's running it.

In Episode 20, Katie Reusch, Director of Youth Programs at YSA (Youth Service America) [at the time of filming], explained how youth-led grant recipients design their projects to include volunteerism and leadership. A strong design often includes the people behind it.

Strategic Budgeting

Another subject-matter expert, Matt Berkowitz, Founder of All Set PEO Consultants (Episode 19), discussed why Professional Employer Organizations (PEOs) matter to nonprofits and small businesses. When designing organizational budgets, fringe benefit costs must also be accounted for.

According to Matt Berkowitz, "What a PEO does, in its essence, is it allows companies to take their payroll, their HR, or ...parts of HR, as well as their benefits and health insurance, and put it all into one solution."

Matt Berkowitz explained further that, "The main benefit for many nonprofits and small businesses is that when they go shopping for health insurance, the rates are often very expensive. A Professional Employer Organization allows small groups to come together into one larger group." According to Matt, "This gives better buying power and potentially much lower cost to add to your budget."

Insights from Grant Funders

Sometimes the best insights come from what funders wish more applicants knew. Laurel Meleski, Director of Operations at RedRover (Episode 27), explained that she often sees strong programs with weak applications because people rush or don't read instructions. Taking time to get it right can make all the difference.

Karren Timmermans, President and Executive Director of The Pilcrow Foundation (Episode 24), reminded applicants that it's okay to reach out and ask questions. Her team wants applicants to succeed, and a thoughtful question before submission can improve a proposal's chances.

In Episode 36, Sarah Lyding, Executive Director of The Music Man Foundation, emphasized the foundation's focus on grants for systemic, permanent change in arts funding.

"We make grants to programs that are bridging music, well-being, and learning. We have a grant program for advocacy and work that impacts policy, policy that would affect the arts sector or increase public funding for the arts, and then we make some grants in honor of Meredith and Rosemary Willson's musical legacy." By prioritizing advocacy and policy, The Music Man Foundation teaches organizations how to embed arts into core systems to withstand budget cuts.

These insights from funders highlight the bigger picture, but they also underscore a practical starting point: building your proposal around a solid budget.

Build Your Grant on a Solid Foundation

Before diving into writing, start with the budget. Funders want to see exactly how their money will be used, and a well-organized budget ensures that the proposal aligns with their priorities. A clear budget also helps applicants structure their narrative, demonstrating that they have thought through the project's costs and sustainability (Episodes 1 and 6).

Beyond numbers, a strong budget tells a story. Eloiza Altoro (Episode 48) explained, "We pay for consultants to come in and do the work. A lot of nonprofits don't have the funds, or they might not necessarily receive funding from groups that would allow that. So we pay for consultants to come in and support them in some of these capacity areas that they might need as far as smaller types of projects."

It shows funders that the organization understands financial planning, has realistic expectations, and can manage grant funds responsibly. Many applicants focus too much on the narrative, leaving budgeting as an afterthought. Funders emphasize that the budget is equally important to making a strong case (Episodes 1 and 6).

Prove You're Ready to Deliver

You can't just say you're ready; you must show it. In Episode 2, David Proebstel, Treasurer of the Sequim City Band, explained how they laid out every detail of their proposal: the concert timeline, rehearsal schedule, and community partnerships. It proved Sequim City Band wasn't just dreaming; they were ready to deliver.

Melanie Reeves, Executive Director of RiverLife (Episode 47), shared, "By the end of 2024, we had completed all five ramps with our volunteer groups."

Start with Need: Grant Writing Out of Necessity

So many of the organizations I spoke with didn't get into grant writing because they wanted to. They did it because they had to. Melanie Reeves, Executive Director of RiverLife (Episode 47), said, "It is really out of necessity, honestly."

Melanie Reeves saw how many people needed wheelchair ramps and basic home repairs, and there just wasn't enough help. Her team jumped into grant writing to meet that urgent demand.

Homer Bizzle III, President and CEO of America Cares Too (Episode 44), a veteran himself, founded his nonprofit after realizing he could step up to help veterans with food, housing, and mental health support. These aren't abstract needs; they're real, and they pushed him to act.

Turning Rejection into Opportunity

Getting a rejection doesn't mean the door is closed forever. Many funders encourage applicants to seek feedback and refine their proposals for future submissions. Grant applications are competitive, and even strong proposals can miss out simply due to limited funds. The key is persistence: learn from past mistakes and keep applying. (Episodes 3 and 8).

Organizations that take the time to ask funders why they were denied and modify their proposals often succeed in future cycles. Many funders appreciate applicants who demonstrate growth and may even invite them to reapply. A well-improved resubmission demonstrates dedication and adaptability, both of which funders respect (Episodes 3 and 8).

Not every great idea gets funded right away. In Episode 4, Dina Ray, Director of Development at But God Ministries, described how they faced early rejections but kept refining their model. Today, they've built entire communities in the Mississippi Delta, with clinics, housing, schools, and clean water.

Applicants can use their past proposals as templates for future opportunities. A rejected proposal doesn't need to go to waste.

Alexis Hyde, Director of Art and Outreach, Quinn Emanuel Urquhart & Sullivan, LLP (Trial Lawyers), gave some straight talk in Episode 40 about not giving up after a rejection: "If you don't get something, you are in incredible, incredible company. The people that I have had to turn away are incredible artists, and you're in incredible company. It doesn't necessarily mean that you're not a good artist, or that it's a reflection on you in any way. It just means it wasn't the right fit at the right time. I say apply again. As I said, I'm getting hundreds of applications. Apply every single time. You don't even necessarily need to change the application. Keep applying. I've had,

I'm not going to name names, but one of the artists applied....they didn't get it until [after applying] multiple times, and they applied with the same application every single time."

My advice is to keep applying; the right fit might come next time, even if you submit the same application.

What Happens If You Don't Get Funded?

Building on how to turn rejection around, let's get practical about what to do next, because a 'no' is often just the start of a stronger yes.

Let's be honest, not every application ends in a win. But here's the good news: "No" doesn't mean "Never." It usually means "Not this time."

My children think that "No" means "Maybe." That's why they ask again.

Rejection is part of the process, but it's not the end of the road. Laurel Meleski from RedRover (Episode 27) shared that many grantees who were turned down the first time came back stronger after they asked for feedback.

Some organizations take the time to provide feedback to every applicant and encourage them to come back. Laurel Meleski,

Director of Operations at RedRover (Episode 27), offers pre-application support for reapplicants, and Traci Lanier, Vice President at 10,000 Degrees (Episode 21), turned a rejection into a mentorship opportunity.

Traci Lanier from 10,000 Degrees (Episode 21) reminded us that even a "no" can lead to a relationship. Some of their funders initially said no but appreciated the follow-up, saw the organization grow, and later came on board.

The key is to ask for feedback, revise, and get back in the game. Sometimes, you were number 16 on a list of 15 winners. So, keep your calendar handy and your draft in progress.

Beyond mindset, here are practical ways to turn rejection into future success.

Follow Up After Rejection

A rejected application is not the end of the road. Many organizations successfully receive funding after resubmitting improved proposals. Funders may offer valuable feedback or suggest alternative funding sources that better align with an organization's mission (Episodes 8 and 4).

Feedback Is Fuel

One of the best-kept secrets in grant writing is that funders want you to improve, and they'll help you do it.

Organizations provide written feedback and access to pre-application coaching. Laurel Meleski (Episode 27) walks applicants through proposals to strengthen future rounds.

Soon Hagerty, Co-Founder and President of the Boundless Futures Foundation (Episode 52), even brings in mentors to help founders think through their pitch, product, and strategy, not just their form.

So, if you get feedback, don't take it personally. Take it as a roadmap. Funders don't just want to fund; they want to grow leaders.

Track Your Grants with a Calendar

The best grant writers I know keep a grant calendar, and they stick to it. It's not just for deadlines. It's for reminders, prep work, report due dates, and application windows.

GrantWatch always had a grant calendar for subscribers. With the new technology available in 2026, GrantWatch enhanced the "My Grant Calendar" to be fully downloadable to your personal calendar in Outlook, Yahoo, or Google. It is a great feature and fully explained in Chapter 4.

As I always say: apply, apply, apply! But to do that, you've got to know when and where to apply. Start a spreadsheet. Use sticky notes. Print a wall calendar. Whatever works for you, just keep track.

And don't toss a grant deadline after one rejection. Traci Lanier, Vice President at 10,000 Degrees (Episode 21), said, "Reapplying is expected and encouraged." Next year could be your year.

Apply, Apply, Apply

Every grant you apply for is a learning experience. Traci Lanier, Vice President at 10,000 Degrees (Episode 21), shared how some of their best funding relationships started with a rejection. They kept applying, built connections, and eventually earned trust. If you're not successful the first time, that doesn't mean you won't be the next time.

Magda Galindo, Director of Grants Management at FFAR (the Foundation for Food & Agriculture Research), shared some encouraging words in Episode 41 for people considering grant applications. "I think you don't lose anything by trying, right?... And I think that... if you see an opportunity... it is something that you're interested in, or something that your organization does, but you're not certain where to start. Reach out to us."

Magda continued, "You know, we can help you... FFAR is very unique with... the partnerships we have. If you don't know, if you have the match, reach out to us. We may be able to assist or at least guide you in the right direction. And then also... just stay up with everything that we do. Sign up for our newsletter, check our website, look at the projects we have funded to see if it's something... not the same, obviously, but similar, or just to look at the ideas that have received funding, so you can see how innovative our projects may be. And just don't be shy....If it fits within our 'Priority Areas', we're interested. And if it's something we end up not funding, we will tell you why and, hopefully, create an opportunity, either back at FFAR or elsewhere.... But always be on the lookout."

Magda Galindo emphasized, "Always be in the know, and with GrantWatch... You have the opportunities at your fingertips."

Always ask questions if you're stuck and keep an eye on what's out there.

Finding the Right Grant

Check GrantWatch regularly because we add new grants every day, and you might find the perfect fit.

There are so many grants out there, but not all of them are the right fit for you. The trick is knowing where to look and how to tell which opportunities line up with your mission.

Getting Ready to Apply

Before you even open a grant application, there's work to do. Some of the strongest advice I heard in these interviews had nothing to do with writing and everything to do with being ready when the right grant comes along.

Lisa Evangelos, the National Administrator of the Culinary Federation of Canada, in Episode 35, said, "Don't rush to meet a deadline. If you have time, create a calendar and look to the future."

Customize While Staying Organized

While having reusable grant templates can save time, customization is key. A one-size-fits-all approach does not work in grant writing. Adjusting proposals to meet each funder's unique requirements increases the likelihood of success (Episodes 12 and 31).

Helena Kosoff, Grant Writer (Episode 23), encourages grant writers to create templates but to always customize them. Keep a library of past proposals, but never send one without editing. Make sure the funder's name, priorities, and language are reflected throughout.

Some Grants Fund the Program, Not the Service

Rachel Roth, Senior Director of Grants & Programs at the Foundation for Financial Planning (Episode 45), explained that their grants do not pay for financial planners themselves. Instead, funding supports the infrastructure required to run a pro bono financial planning program, including staff time, volunteer recruitment, training, coordination, and program management, while CERTIFIED FINANCIAL PLANNER ® professionals donate their services at no cost.

As Jessica Safransky Schacht, COO of United Way of Racine County, explained in Episode 32, funders like United Way focus on targeted impact. "We fund programs, not organizations, meaning we have a set of established outcomes and indicators that we use to collectively track progress towards those outcomes. Organizations then decide which of their programs could help contribute to some collective impact in our community. And then they propose programs for funding that way."

This approach ensures grants align with community-wide goals and measurable results.

Know Where to Look

If you don't know where to start, you're not alone. Many first-time grant seekers find the process overwhelming. Brenda Swann, Director of Grants and Operations at the St. Johns County Cultural Council (Episode 22), shared that many of their applicants learn about arts and tourism funding through direct outreach and grant listings. Don't just rely on search engines, check trusted platforms, talk to your local arts council, and sign up for alerts.

Expand Your Search for Opportunities

One of the most common mistakes grant seekers make is searching too narrowly. Many grants fall under broader or unexpected funding areas, and missing these opportunities can limit an organization's funding potential. Funders suggest using a variety of search terms and expanding research to include lesser-known funding sources (Episodes 4 and 12).

Organizations that invest time in diversifying their grant search tend to find more success. Instead of focusing solely on direct program funding, consider grants for capacity building, technology upgrades, or general operating support. Many funders are open to flexible funding, but applicants must be strategic in how they present their needs (Episodes 4 and 12).

Don't stop after one search. Samantha Walters, CEO and former Senior Strategist at Colocation America (Episode 25), encourages applicants to keep looking for grants that fit, not just in the obvious places. Her team specifically looks for applicants who are doing innovative work in STEM education and often finds grant programs through less-traditional channels. Be open-minded and persistent (Episode 41).

GrantWatch offers multiple search capabilities through dropdowns and AI search.

Grant Writing Is a Team Effort

While many organizations rely on a single grant writer, the most successful applications involve collaboration. Finance teams, program directors, and leadership should all contribute their expertise to ensure the proposal is accurate and well-rounded. Funders can tell when an application has been written in isolation rather than reflecting the full scope of an organization's work (Episodes 6 and 10).

Having different team members involved also ensures that all details align, particularly between the budget and the narrative.

Funders frequently encounter applications in which financial projections don't align with the written proposal, raising red flags. A cohesive, well-prepared submission stands out and builds credibility (Episodes 25 and 41).

Capacity Building Starts from Within

Grants can help you grow, but real capacity building starts internally.

Eloiza Altoro, Fund Advisor at the Nonprofit Management Fund (Episode 48), said, "Our focus is around capacity building for nonprofits... governance, training, leadership, financial management, fund development, and marketing communications."

A director of a community foundation (Episode 26) discussed how they help small nonprofits grow by making the grant process collaborative. Their community grant program allows multiple funders to review and co-fund a single application. This approach not only reduces the burden on applicants but also teaches them how to work within funding systems.

Nobody does this alone. Even small organizations found ways to bring people together to write grants. Melanie Reeves, Executive Director of RiverLife (Episode 47), told us that when writing the grant, the executive director, the Board chair, and the office manager all pitched in.

In Episode 6, Katy Sursa, Director of Community Development at United Cerebral Palsy of Arkansas, had her whole staff backing her up when she wrote that big transportation grant. Grant writing can be intimidating, but when you do it as a team, it's also empowering.

As these stories show, internal strength through teamwork sets the stage for external success by starting with manageable wins.

Start Small, Build Credibility

Funders often advise new grant seekers to start with smaller grants before applying for large-scale funding. Organizations with a track record of managing smaller grants successfully are more attractive candidates for major funding opportunities. Melanie Reeves, Executive Director (Episode 47), said RiverLife received "$4,500 to build five ramps" and completed the project within the grant period.

Demonstrating responsible use of funds and completing projects builds trust with funders (Episodes 2 and 31).

This approach also allows organizations to refine their grant writing skills. A series of small wins adds up and strengthens an organization's reputation. Many large funders review an applicant's grant history, so showing a steady progression of secured funding can work in an organization's favor (Episodes 2 and 31).

Eligibility and Structure Matter

Brenda Swann from the St. Johns County Cultural Council (Episode 22) emphasized the importance of checking eligibility before applying. Some grants are limited by geography, budget size, or organization type. In Episode 38, Dr. Allison Hamilton Molnar, Executive Director of CNTA (Citizens for Nuclear Technology Awareness), said that structure matters just as much as content. A sloppy budget or an incomplete application can be disqualifying.

Follow the Rules, Every Time

Every funder has different application guidelines, and failing to follow them is one of the quickest ways to get disqualified. Eloiza Altoro, Fund Advisor at Nonprofit Management Fund (Episode 48), said, "That's the biggest faux pas, applying for a grant and having absolutely no idea what you're applying for. At least read the website and eligibility requirements."

Some funders require specific formatting, word counts, or supporting documents. Missing even a minor requirement can prevent an application from being reviewed. Carefully reading all the instructions can make the difference between approval and rejection (Episodes 8 and 12).

Funders have noted that some organizations submit strong proposals that, unfortunately, are never considered simply because they fail to meet a technical requirement. Double-checking eligibility criteria, required attachments, and deadlines ensures that all the hard work that you put into a proposal isn't wasted (Episodes 8 and 12).

Lisa-Marie Haygood, Executive Director of the Cherokee County Educational Foundation (Episode 30), explained that her foundation redacts identifying information to ensure grants are reviewed fairly. But if someone ignores the instructions or misses a deadline, they're out of the running. No matter how great the project is, rules are rules.

Make the First Move: Contact the Funder

Here's something I tell people all the time: don't wait to apply before you talk to the funder. If they respond, you are in luck and can get valuable help. But do not miss a deadline for a grant that you deem you are eligible for.

Eloiza Altoro (Episode 48) said, "We allow for one-on-one consultations... It's an opportunity for them to ask if what they're pitching would fit within our funding guidelines."

Elisabeth Kruger, Manager of Arctic Wildlife at World Wildlife Fund (Episode 50), explained that applicants are encouraged to email or call before applying, noting that her role is intentionally structured to help people shape their ideas and guide them through the application process.

You can, and should, make the first move. Some of the best advice from funders came down to this simple idea: introduce yourself early and stay in touch.

Helen Kosoff, Grant Writer (Episode 23), had a great tip: even if you're not sure you're ready to apply, reach out. Funders appreciate it when applicants take the time to ask questions first. You gain clarity, and they hear your organization's name before the proposal even lands.

Samantha Walters, CEO and former Senior Strategist at Colocation America (Episode 25), shared that they even host "lunch and learn" calls to walk applicants through their STEM Innovation Grant. These optional calls often lead to stronger proposals and give the funder a chance to hear directly from potential applicants.

Keep Funders in the Loop

Winning a grant isn't just about securing funding; it's about building a long-term relationship. Funders appreciate it when grantees provide updates on their progress, even outside the required reporting periods. Keeping funders informed about successes, challenges, and organizational growth increases the likelihood of future funding (Episodes 10, 21, and 30).

Funders want to see impact beyond just numbers. Sharing stories, testimonials, and lessons learned from grant-funded projects demonstrates transparency and accountability. Many funders consider past grantee relationships when awarding new grants, so maintaining open communication can lead to multi-year support (Episodes 10 and 21).

Once you've made contact, don't go silent. Keep funders updated, even if you haven't applied yet. Lisa-Marie Haygood from the Cherokee County Educational Foundation (Episode 30) said she loves it when past applicants check in, send photos, or share outcomes. It shows commitment and builds long-term trust.

And don't forget, relationships matter. In Episode 21, Traci Lanier from 10,000 Degrees talked about how staying connected with funders led to unexpected support, even from those who initially said no.

Transparency and Honest Communication

Ryanne Jennings, President and CEO of the Wayne County Community Foundation (Episode 39), encourages applicants to communicate like real people. "We're not just funders, we're partners," she said. Rejections happen, but if you've built a relationship, it's easier to try again. She reminds us that a "no" today might be a "yes" next cycle.

Tim Tramble, Sr., President and CEO of Saint Luke's Foundation (Episode 37), put it this way: "Funders want to support people who are doing real work, not just writing polished proposals. The more human your communication is, the more likely funders are to connect with your mission."

Honesty about organizational limitations fosters trust with funders. If your organization does not meet every funding requirement, addressing those challenges openly while proposing solutions demonstrates integrity and adaptability (Episodes 23 and 10).

Every organization has limits, and that's okay. What matters is being honest about them. In Episode 39, Ryanne Jennings, President and CEO of the Wayne County Community Foundation, encourages applicants not to give up after a rejection. Often, it's not about the proposal being bad; it's about timing or available funds.

In Episode 38, Dr. Hamilton Molnar explains that a great idea can still be passed over if the application doesn't show how the project can sustain itself. Transparency builds trust.

It's okay not to have all the answers. Funders aren't looking for perfect; they're looking for honesty. Eloiza Altoro (Episode 48) said, "We're not looking for perfect organizations. It's okay to be open and honest about challenges, that's how we can support them."

Laurel Meleski, Director of Operations at RedRover (Episode 27), discussed how her team responds well to applicants who clearly explain their limitations. When they know your challenges, they can be more flexible with their support.

And in Episode 26, a director of a community foundation explained that their multi-funder model makes even partial funding possible, but only if applicants are upfront about what they really need.

Funders as Partners, Not Paper Pushers

In Episode 13, Sarah Roberts, Director of the Connie Dwyer Breast Cancer Foundation, shared that they want more than just paperwork; they want a partnership. They appreciate updates, photos, and even mid-project check-ins. They're looking for grantees who see them as collaborators.

We heard in Episode 35 how The Culinary Federation received $25,000 in funding from the City of Saskatoon post-COVID to bring together chefs, cooks, and culinary partners all across Canada, from Vancouver to the coast.

The foundation in (Episode 29) told us that they work closely with grantees after funding to help ensure the project's success. It's not just about the check; it's about shared outcomes.

Personalization Wins Over Generic Submissions

A common mistake applicants make is copying and pasting the same proposal for multiple funders. While templates can be useful, each application should be tailored to reflect the specific funder's goals and priorities. Funders easily recognize when an application has been customized or mass-submitted (Episodes 21 and 23).

Taking the time to personalize proposals not only increases the likelihood of funding but also demonstrates genuine interest in the funder's mission. Showing how an organization's work aligns with the funder's objectives strengthens an application and makes it stand out (Episodes 21 and 23).

Generic proposals rarely win. Samantha Walters from Colocation America (Episode 25) explained that they are looking for applicants who clearly explain what makes their program different. Their reviewers want to see the connection between the grant and your unique approach, not a cut-and-paste submission.

A foundation that deals with a specific niche industry (Episode 29) said that the strongest proposals they receive speak directly to their mission. If you're applying for research funding, they want to see that you understand the industry and can explain why your project matters to the field.

Highlighting what sets your program apart is crucial, but funders also need evidence to support it. That's where data comes in (Episodes 12 and 25).

Data-Driven Needs Statements Make a Difference

A compelling "needs statement" backed by data strengthens a proposal. Funders look for measurable outcomes and clear justifications for why a project deserves funding. Including relevant statistics and case studies provides credibility and increases the likelihood of securing support (Episodes 6 and 31).

Funders want to help, but they need to see the facts. In Episode 38, Dr. Allison Hamilton Molnar, Director of CNTA, discussed the need for solid data in proposals. She wanted to know how many people a program would serve and how success would be measured.

And in Episode 39, Ryanne Jennings, President and CEO of the Wayne County Community Foundation, said they review proposals for cost-effectiveness and long-term impact. Your passion is important, but numbers help tell the full story.

To put this data-driven approach into practice, let's focus on crafting a needs statement that grabs attention from the start.

Crafting a Strong Needs Statement

When you're writing a grant, your needs statement is your first impression. It's your chance to tell the funder, "Here's what's happening on the ground, and here's why it matters." This isn't the place for buzzwords or lofty mission language. It's the moment to show what your community is lacking, who's affected, and what will change if you're funded.

Funders like Dr. Allison Hamilton Molnar at CNTA (Episode 38) told me they're looking for numbers and narratives. How many people are you serving? What's your evidence? Ryanne Jennings (Episode 39) said proposals that were tied to measurable outcomes stood out. So, give your needs statement some heart, but also ground it in data.

A solid needs statement gets your foot in the door, but to keep the momentum going, visibility through public relations can turn one-time funding into ongoing support (Episodes 12, 25, and 29).

Building Visibility Through Public Relations

Nonprofits often have impactful programs, but without visibility, potential donors, volunteers, and partners may never know about them. Public relations can bridge that gap and support long-term funding success.

As Sandy Collier, PR Professional at Hey, Sandy! PR & Communications, explained in Episode 34, visibility is essential for nonprofits to secure community funding. "Nonprofits rely on getting funding from the community... for the community to help them with their programs or what they're doing, the community needs to know what they're doing... And I always tell a lot of nonprofit businesses, you can't afford to not have PR... if you have the best program in the world, but if nobody knows who you are, then what's the point?"

Building awareness through PR can lead to increased donations and partnerships. Preparation matters just as much for PR as it does for grants.

In Episode 34, Sandy Collier stressed the importance of preparation before engaging PR services. "One thing you need to understand is [that] not all people who want PR are ready for it... Just like with grants, you have to get ready for it... You're not ready for me yet. You need to go and get all your thoughts in a row... Decide exactly what you're going to offer, how you're going to do it, all of that."

This mirrors the process of becoming grant-ready, ensuring organizations are positioned for success.

Storytelling lies at the heart of effective PR for nonprofits. "I love creating stories... I consider myself a reporter's friend... I give the reporter everything in a one-stop shopping... It's a great package, a great story that people can look at... I love telling stories that matter... stories that can help other people."

Compelling narratives can attract media attention and drive support for grant-seeking efforts. By investing in PR when ready, nonprofits can amplify their mission, build credibility, and create a stronger foundation for sustained funding.

By building this visibility, you're not just preparing to apply for grants; you're setting up for what comes next once the funding is in hand (Episodes 29 and 31).

After You're Funded

Getting the grant is a major milestone, but it's also the beginning of a new phase. What you do after you're funded can set the stage for future grants, stronger relationships, and bigger impact.

Soon Hagerty (Episode 52) shared that Boundless Futures Foundation pairs funding with hands-on support. Grant recipients receive their funds quickly, but more importantly, they gain access to a year-long advisory circle covering finance, branding, scaling, and leadership, reinforcing that capacity building doesn't stop once the check clears.

This kind of ongoing support strengthens grantees, but it also highlights a broader truth. The strongest funding relationships are built over time through consistent communication and trust (Episodes 10, 26, and 30).

Strong Relationships Lead to Continued Funding

Engaging with funders beyond the grant application process increases the chances of securing future support. Regular interactions, site-visit invitations, and sharing impact reports help establish trust and credibility. This often leads to multi-year commitments (Episodes 21 and 3).

Brenda Swann from the St. Johns County Cultural Council (Episode 22) explained that most of their grantees return each year because of good communication and clear reporting. Funders notice when you keep them in the loop and share progress.

Karren Timmermans, President and Executive Director of The Pilcrow Foundation (Episode 24), shared how rural libraries that report back with photos and host celebrations become stronger candidates for future awards. It's about more than the report; it's about the relationship.

Strong communication and reporting not only secure future funding but also reflect a broader trend. Many funders now offer training and coaching to help applicants succeed from the start.

Use Resources: Training Is Available

Helena Kosoff, Grant Writer (Episode 23), suggested that new grant writers take advantage of reviewer training opportunities.

Katie Reusch, Director of Youth Programs at YSA (Youth Service America) [at the time of filming] (Episode 20), also mentioned that her organization provides coaching and guidance to youth grantees because no one is expected to figure it out alone.

Pre-Application Coaching: Use It!

If a funder offers help before you even apply, take it. That's like getting the answer key before the test.

Patty Eljaiek, Long Island Grants for the Arts Coordinator for Huntington Arts Council (Episode 49), explained that every applicant is offered one-on-one mentorship, including scheduled calls to discuss eligibility, criteria, and how a project fits the grant, because helping artists apply well is part of the mission.

Elisabeth Kruger, Manager of Arctic Wildlife at World Wildlife Fund (Episode 50), shared that their competitive grant program was designed to remove barriers to applying, emphasizing that funders are primarily interested in the idea and its impact, not perfect writing, and that coaching is available to help applicants explain how their project will work.

In Episode 32, Jessica Safransky Schacht described how United Way of Racine County builds equity through supportive processes. "We instituted some things like a mandatory pre-application meeting where we just sat with the organization and had a conversation to really hear what their idea was. And then, from there, give them some pointers on the proposal itself." This hands-on guidance helps grassroots groups succeed and reflects a shift toward collaborative funding.

In Episode 42, a program officer at a library foundation described how their application process includes a webinar support series for applicants invited to submit a final proposal. The sessions bring in subject-matter experts to walk applicants through complex elements of the application, such as rights, ethics and reuse, budgeting and finance, and collection assessment. The webinars give applicants the chance to ask questions directly to experts and the grants team, and recordings, transcripts, and Q&A documents are later posted online, including on YouTube, as ongoing resources.

Watching past webinars like these can help you navigate through tricky sections and build a stronger proposal.

When you're not sure you're the right fit, reach out. Karren Timmermans, President and Executive Director of The Pilcrow Foundation (Episode 24), told me she answers questions before applications come because she wants people to succeed.

Don't go it alone. Coaching is part of the opportunity.

Learn from the Inside Out

Beyond direct coaching from funders, you can also gain powerful insight by stepping into the reviewer's seat or studying successful examples.

The best way to grow as a grant writer is to learn how reviewers think. Helena Kosoff, Grant Writer (Episode 23), strongly recommends volunteering as a grant reviewer. Whether through AmeriCorps, foundations, or government grant agencies, volunteering as a reviewer can give you an inside look at what makes a proposal work and where people fall short.

Katie Reusch, Director of Youth Programs at YSA Youth Service America [at time of filming] (Episode 20), talked about how many of their youth applicants improve by reading sample proposals and learning from each other's drafts. It's a skill you build with practice.

In Episode 42, a program officer from a library foundation highlighted the importance of gaining experience as a grant reviewer. Some foundations periodically invite people to express interest in serving on review panels, sometimes as volunteers and sometimes with a stipend. Sitting on these panels offers a behind-the-scenes look at how funding decisions are made.

Signing up to review grants lets you see exactly what makes a proposal stand out and strengthens your own applications.

Prepare Financial Documents in Advance

Incomplete or inaccurate financial documents can derail an otherwise strong application. Ensuring that budgets, audits, and financial statements are updated and ready before applying saves time and prevents last-minute issues (Episodes 35 and 6).

Disaster Relief: Prepare Before It Happens

Karren Timmermans, President and Executive Director of The Pilcrow Foundation (Episode 24), explained that their emergency grants for libraries affected by disasters such as floods or fires go to those who are already prepared. That means keeping inventories, tracking books, and having a response plan. Plan for disaster recovery before the disaster hits.

Get Ready Before the Grant Drops

The worst time to scramble for your budget or board list is the night before the deadline. Start now, before the grant even goes live.

Brenda Swann (Episode 22) and Dr. Allison Hamilton Molnar (Episode 38) both stressed the importance of financial readiness. Do you have your 990 filed? Do you know your cost per client served? These are the basics that funders expect.

I have seen training start 2 to 3 months before the application. Prepare as if the opportunity is already here, because it will be.

This kind of preparation pays off when that first opportunity arrives, as many of my guests discovered through their initial successes.

First Grant Successes

Organizations often start small, securing initial grants that pave the way for future funding. Whether it was a $7,500 grant from the Pennsylvania Department of Agriculture (Episode 1) or a $1,000 award from the Disaster Relief International Foundation (Episode 3), these early wins built momentum.

Some organizations, such as UCP of Arkansas, secured significant initial grants, including a $170,000 Department of Transportation grant for vans for people with disabilities (Episode 6).

Others, like But God Ministries, leveraged GrantWatch to secure a $10,000 grant for wheelchair ramps (Episode 4). These initial successes not only provided crucial funding but also built credibility for future applications.

Celebrate Your First Win: Leverage Future Grants

These early wins aren't just about the money. They're steppingstones, as these recipients shared.

Your first grant isn't just funding success; it's proof of concept. Katy Sursa from United Cerebral Palsy of Arkansas (Episode 6) used her first major win to build confidence and apply again. That first success helped her secure accessible vans and proved her organization could manage larger grants.

In Episode 8, Steven Silver, Philanthropic Advisor at Philanthropic Services of the Southwest and former Grants Manager at CRIT TeletonUSA, explained how a grant allowed them to expand services for children with disabilities.

In Episode 10, Wayne Jackson, Executive Director of Mercy Medical Free Clinics, shared how securing a grant, through GrantWatch, helped them scale care for uninsured patients. These stories show that getting one grant can help unlock many more.

Model What Works and Multiply It

In Episode 1, Mary Jane Taylor, Director of Grants and Research at Williamson College of the Trades, explained how they grew their vocational training model into a replicable success story. Funders love it when an idea can be expanded, adapted, or scaled. If your program works, show how it could work elsewhere.

Recipients Benefiting from GrantWatch

For many, these first successes came through resources like GrantWatch, which helped organizations turn preparation into real impact.

On the recipient side, Bobbi Donovan, President and CEO of Sunshine Family Outreach Center (Episode 14), shared how securing a bookmobile grant through GrantWatch had a significant impact on their literacy programming in North Highlands, California. That one grant helped them expand services to kids who had no regular access to books.

How GrantWatch Helps

GrantWatch has played a pivotal role in helping organizations find funders they would not have otherwise considered. Some, like the Sequim City Band, used filtering tools to identify arts-related funding opportunities (Episode 2).

Dina Ray (Episode 4) recently wrote a direct quote for me to include in this book. I remember her saying this during the interview as well. I am very grateful to Dina for her support: "But God Ministries appreciates the ease of finding grants and connecting with funders using GrantWatch's software. It is an affordable tool that pays for itself with just one successful grant. This software has helped take BGM from an organization that had never received a grant in 2018 to one that has now received over $4,000,000 in grants."

Others, such as Mercy Medical Free Clinics, relied on it as a database to track potential funding sources (Episode 10). Organizations have successfully secured multiple grants using GrantWatch, with some reporting that their first grant through the platform covered the subscription cost multiple times over (Episode 3). Its ability to provide regular email notifications and streamline searches has made it an invaluable resource for nonprofits and grant seekers alike (Episodes 4 and 12). Several guests found success by using GrantWatch to discover new opportunities.

Appearing on the GrantWatch GrantTalk podcast has had a positive effect on nonprofits. Right before this book, *The Queen of Grants 2* went to print, I received the following email from Homer Lee Bizzle III, M.A. Ed., President and CEO of America Cares Too: "Thank you for the opportunity to participate on your podcast. Following our discussion, I am pleased to share that America Cares Too was awarded a $250,000 grant from the State of Illinois Department of Human Services (IDHS) for our Employment & Training Enhanced Services Program....Thank you again for providing America Cares Too with the platform to share our mission with your audience."

Funders Using GrantWatch

It's not just applicants who benefit. Funders (Episode 29) also use GrantWatch. Foundations use listings like those on GrantWatch to reach scientific researchers and nonprofit partners nationwide.

Listing your grant where people are already looking makes a big difference. It helps ensure that your funding opportunities are visible to qualified applicants who are actively searching for grants.

Karren Timmermans, President and Executive Director of The Pilcrow Foundation (Episode 24), said that after they listed their rural library grant on GrantWatch, they saw a noticeable jump in applications, from areas they'd never reached before. The platform helped them get the word out to the right people.

Tools like GrantWatch can open doors, but sustaining success often comes down to overcoming hurdles through strong, ongoing relationships, as many guests shared.

Overcoming Obstacles & Nurturing Relationships

Fundraising is not without its challenges; organizations that build strong relationships with funders often achieve continued success. Rosaline Bangura of Be Rose International Foundation told us how they achieved long-term funding from the Community Foundation of Anne Arundel County by maintaining open communication (Episode 3).

Guest House Chicago emphasized that relationship-building led to consistent year-over-year funding renewals (Episode 7).

Meanwhile, UCP of Arkansas faced a difficult period of multiple grant rejections but found persistence key to ultimately securing funding (Episode 6). Following up with funders after rejection often leads to new opportunities, as many organizations have received in-kind support or suggestions for alternative funding (Episode 4).

Understanding funders' priorities and tailoring applications accordingly can also increase the chances of success (Episodes 8 and 21).

Tailoring your needs to funders' priorities is key, but the most effective approaches go further by considering the full spectrum of community needs.

Think Holistically About Community Needs

The most successful funded programs don't just fix one problem; they look at the bigger picture. Elisabeth Kruger, Manager of Arctic Wildlife at World Wildlife Fund (Episode 50), explained that funders are not embedded in communities' day-to-day and rely on applicants to surface local concerns, making listening to them a central part of their grantmaking approach.

In Episode 4, But God Ministries explained that they work to build sustainable communities in difficult places through their model, SPHERES. This model focuses on Spiritual, Physical (Medical and

Dental), H2O, Education, Roofs (Housing), Economic Development (Jobs), and Soil (Access to Healthy Food) because all these areas affect a community's quality of life.

Financial Literacy as Program Component

One way to address these interconnected needs is to incorporate practical skills such as financial literacy, as this guest illustrated.

Eloiza Altoro, Fund Advisor of the Nonprofit Management Fund (Episode 48), explained how her organization builds financial literacy into its workforce development programs. When funders saw that they were helping people not just get jobs but manage their money, it added long-term value.

Adding elements like financial literacy reflects a deeper trend in funding, one that several guests described as trust-based philanthropy.

Trust-Based Philanthropy: What It Really Means

This term came up more than once, but it's more than just talk. Funders are shifting how they build relationships with grantees.

Tim Tramble, Sr., President & CEO of Saint Luke's Foundation (Episode 37), talked about funding grassroots organizations that are deeply connected to their communities. His organization cares more about impact than polished proposals. He called their form of philanthropy "trust-based philanthropy" and "participatory philanthropy," funding rooted in relationships, respect, and shared purpose.

The takeaway? You don't have to be the biggest or most professional-looking org. You just have to be authentic, accountable, and aligned.

This emphasis on authenticity opens doors for organizations with big visions, as many grant recipients shared when discussing their next steps.

Grant Recipients' Future Goals

Many organizations have ambitious goals that require strategic funding.

Rosaline Bangura of Be Rose International Foundation aims to secure a $1 million grant to expand its initiatives in Nigeria and Sierra Leone (Episode 3). UCP of Arkansas is working toward sustainable funding to improve employee wages (Episode 6).

Adam Helman, Executive Director of Guest House of Chicago, hopes to broaden its reach, providing housing support to more medical patients (Episode 7).

According to Karen Harvey, Grant Writer at Westminster at Wade (DBA Wade Center), some organizations, such as the Wade Center, are focusing on building endowments to ensure long-term sustainability (Episode 31).

Others, such as 10,000 Degrees, aim to expand scholarships to support more first-generation college students (Episode 21). These aspirations highlight the critical role of ongoing fundraising efforts in maximizing nonprofit impact.

The best proposals hint at what's next. In Episode 1, Director of Grants and Research Mary-Jane Taylor from Williamson College of the Trades talked about scaling their model to help more students nationwide.

And in Episode 17, Elliot Rosenfeld, President and CEO of Net Is Up, explained how his tech company is building partnerships to expand cybersecurity training for nonprofits. Growth, vision, and collaboration make funders want to stick with you.

These ambitious plans succeed when aligned with what funders truly value. Let's dive deeper into their perspectives for even more guidance.

The Grant Vetting Process

Drawing from the *GrantTalk* episodes, here's a closer look at how funders start their evaluations. Let's begin with the basics.

Funders follow a rigorous process to vet applications before making funding decisions. The first step is ensuring that the applicant meets basic eligibility criteria, such as nonprofit status and compliance with IRS regulations. Organizations that fail to meet these foundational requirements are often filtered out early in the process (Episodes 23 and 29).

Beyond eligibility, funders review applications for alignment with their mission and priorities. This involves assessing the clarity of the proposal, the project's feasibility, and the potential for measurable impact. Some funders use scoring systems to evaluate applications, while others hold panel discussions or invite external experts to weigh in on proposals (Episodes 38 and 39).

Vetting starts before a reviewer even reads your story. A director of a community foundation (Episode 26) said their team checks eligibility, financial standing, and community service history before they pass applications to the next level. That includes ensuring the organization is current on its 990 filings and has a clear track record.

One foundation (Episode 29) emphasized that even well-written proposals can get flagged if the numbers don't add up or if the applicant can't demonstrate readiness to execute the project.

How Funders Make Decisions

Funding decisions are based on a combination of factors, including how well the proposed project aligns with the funder's mission, the organization's track record, and the sustainability of the project. Funders prioritize projects with clear, measurable goals and a strong implementation plan. Competitive grants are often awarded to those who demonstrate long-term community impact (Episodes 12 and 21).

While financial need is a consideration, funders also want to ensure that organizations have the capacity to manage funds effectively. A well-thought-out budget that reflects realistic costs and responsible spending practices significantly improves an application's chances of approval (Episodes 10 and 35).

Brenda Swann, Director of Grants and Operations at the St. Johns County Cultural Council (Episode 22), shared that their panel evaluates both the quality of the program and the organization's financial health. Larger grants are awarded only when an organization demonstrates it can responsibly manage those funds.

Dr. Allison Hamilton Molnar, Executive Director at CNTA (Episode 38), said she looks for proposals with clear outcomes, strong partnerships, and realistic plans. If the goals are vague or the budget doesn't make sense, the application is at risk, no matter how exciting the project sounds.

While strong plans win big awards, don't overlook how smaller grants can build that foundation, as this example shows.

Small Grants Add Up, and Build Real Capacity

Winning one grant is important, but long-term stability often comes from securing multiple smaller grants that support different parts of an organization's work.

Homer Lee Bizzle III, M.A.Ed., President and CEO of America Cares Too (Episode 44), shared that in one year, his organization secured $32,505 in grant funding from multiple foundations, in addition to significant in-kind donations, allowing the organization to address food insecurity, housing referrals, advocacy, and mental health support for veterans and their families.

"GrantWatch had put the icing on top of the cake, locating funders that I had a tough time finding," said Homer Lee Bizzle III (Episode 44).

Rather than relying on a single large award, this approach allowed the organization to build services incrementally while expanding partnerships and credibility.

These layered wins start with crafting proposals that clearly and compellingly showcase your mission.

Writing a Strong Proposal That Stands Out

Writing a strong grant proposal is about more than filling in the blanks. It's about making a clear, compelling case for your work, and doing it in a way that resonates with reviewers who may not know anything about your organization. Here's how to make yours stand out.

Throughout all the interviews, funders repeatedly shared what turns a good application into a funded one. Let's break down the key elements they highlighted most.

A compelling grant proposal tells a clear and engaging story. Funders are drawn to applications that clearly define the problem being addressed, outline achievable goals, and present a detailed execution plan. Providing data to support the proposal strengthens credibility and increases the likelihood of funding (Episodes 11 and 15).

Another key factor is demonstrating how the project will be sustained beyond the grant period. Funders want to invest in projects that will have a lasting impact rather than short-term solutions. A sustainability plan that outlines future funding strategies or community partnerships makes a proposal more appealing (Episodes 11 and 15).

In Episode 5, LaGrand Elliott and Eric Elliott, the two founding members of T.I.M.E. (Together In Mission for Empowerment), talked about how their grant proposal for an urban farming initiative addressed food insecurity, youth employment, and sustainability. What made it memorable was that it didn't just sound good; it was rooted in real need, with a track record and a plan to expand.

Funders take notice of sustainability. And for me, as the interviewer, Episode 5 about T.I.M.E. was one of the most memorable, and I have spoken about it often. Mostly because T.I.M.E. operates like the fish motto: if you teach people to fish, they will always have what to eat, and if you teach people to farm, they will always be able to sustain themselves.

Dr. Cindy Ayers Elliott was unable to attend that day due to a technical issue, but we heard all about how she founded the organization. Her two sons, LaGrand and Eric, told us that they keep applying for grants they locate on GrantWatch, have built a 10-state urban farming program with USDA funding that helps people sustain themselves and their communities through farm-to-table produce and farmers' markets, and that T.I.M.E. now also gives grants.

Think Beyond the Grant: Sustainability and Strategy

Dr. Allison Hamilton Molnar (Episode 38) shared that she looks for long-term vision. Proposals that focus solely on the grant period fail to explain what happens after funding ends. Show your sustainability plan; it matters!

While crafting that long-term vision, many grant writers are turning to modern tools to refine their proposals and streamline the process. This brings us to a timely topic in today's funding landscape: the role of AI in grant writing.

What AI Can, and Can't, Do for You

Let's talk about AI and using it thoughtfully.

In Episode 28, Jason Hill, founder of OWWLL, and other guests discussed how AI can support data research for the needs statement and help users get unstuck when drafting, but not replace the thoughtfulness and mission-centered writing that funders expect. All data needs to be verified. Think of it as a tool, not a shortcut. Since these interviews, AI has continued to advance, and in Chapter

4, we discuss the AI Grant Writing Tool that GrantWatch developed to support intentional writing of section-by-section mapping of needs, goals, objectives, activities, and evaluation for grant seekers.

Tools like ChatGPT can help you organize your thoughts, clean up grammar, and rework a paragraph. But here's what they can't do: bring your passion to life.

Soon Hagerty, Co-Founder and President of the Boundless Futures Foundation (Episode 52), emphasized that her foundation uses video interviews because..."There should be no reason anyone should need to use AI for our applications. We are mostly interested in the idea. We are interested in what you want to achieve and how you want to achieve it."

AI can clean up language, but funders want to interview the thinker, the passionate visionaries. Soon Hagerty (Episode 52) made it clear: her foundation does video interviews because AI can't run your business. It can't fake a mission. It can't speak from the heart.

Use it as a helper, not a writer. Think of AI like a spellchecker or online assistant. But your story and your organization's back story? That must come from you.

If you haven't noticed the details on the cover of this book, you'll see hearts because I truly believe that success: your writing, your ideas, your programming development, and your motivation and intention come from your passion.

Many applications fail simply because they do not follow instructions. Elisabeth Kruger, Manager of Arctic Wildlife at World Wildlife Fund (Episode 50), said her team "received an AI-generated proposal which we did not consider... it was not very coherent and not really on topic." This underscores that AI should never replace original thinking.

Speaking of tools that can trip you up if not used wisely, let's look at some of the most frequent errors funders see in proposals, many of which tie back to skipping basics or leaning too heavily on shortcuts like unedited AI drafts.

Common Mistakes That Lead to Rejection

The most common mistake? Not following directions. Dr. Allison Hamilton Molnar, Executive Director at CNTA (Episode 38), shared that many proposals are rejected simply because required materials are missing or because the application doesn't follow the stated guidelines.

Helena Kosoff, Grant Writer (Episode 23), added that burying key information or failing to answer specific questions is another frequent error. Clear, complete, and compliant applications go further.

Jessica Safransky Schacht from United Way of Racine County highlighted a common pitfall in Episode 32. "One of the biggest mistakes that we see is a lack of continuity or connection between the program activities that are described in the application, the budget that's asking for the resources, and then the proposed outcomes." Applicants can avoid this by mapping their narrative, budget, and evaluation to create a seamless story.

Funders frequently see missing documentation, vague project descriptions, and inconsistencies between the budget and the narrative. Even strong projects can be rejected if the application is incomplete or unclear (Episodes 16, 22, and 48).

Another common mistake is failing to tailor the application to the specific funder. Some applicants submit generic proposals without researching the funder's priorities.

Funders appreciate it when organizations take the time to customize their applications, demonstrating a genuine fit with their mission (Episodes 13, 45, and 52).

How Many Grants Do You Give Out?

This is a question many people are afraid to ask, but you should! Funders usually publish their numbers, and it helps you set realistic expectations.

For example, with about 120 applications received, they may be funding only 5, 10, or 15. When you look in the GrantWatch Foundation Directory, you can see the grants distributed and their amounts for a given year. This may help you trim or expand your request based on the total amount they plan to distribute and their history of grant awards. If they only fund 20 of 120, that doesn't mean the other proposals were bad. It means the money only stretches so far.

Knowing these numbers doesn't mean you don't apply. It just means you go in with your eyes open and ready to stand out.

With that in mind, it's also worth exploring who can apply, because grants aren't limited to big organizations or high-odds competitions.

Some Grants Are for Individuals, Not Just Nonprofits

Most people assume grants are only available to nonprofit organizations, but some funders are structured to provide direct support to individuals as well.

Soon Hagerty (Episode 52) said her foundation awards 4 to 7 grants per quarter to individuals and a single $100,000 grant to a nonprofit each year.

Sharon McGraw, Ed.D., Grant Program Officer at Community Fund Ohio (Episode 43), explained that her organization awards grants directly to individuals with disabilities and to nonprofit organizations serving them in Ohio.

To protect recipients' eligibility for SSI, Medicaid, and other public benefits, Community Fund Ohio does not issue cash grants.

Sharon states clearly that the expense must be directly related to the disability. Payments are made directly to third-party vendors for needs directly related to disability, such as wheelchair ramps, vehicle modifications, therapy, or accessibility improvements.

Individual grants from the Community Fund of Ohio can be awarded up to $7,500, while nonprofit grants can be awarded up to $25,000. The application process is intentionally short and designed to reduce barriers.

When Will You Hear Back?

If you've ever hit "submit" and then stared at your inbox for weeks, you're not alone. Every funder has its own timeline, but most are more transparent than you'd think.

Some funders move fast. Soon Hagerty, at Boundless Futures Foundation (Episode 52), said they try to notify applicants within 30 days.

Ainsley Munro, Coordinator of Trail Infrastructure and Funding, and Heidi Tillmanns, Director of Trail Infrastructure and Funding at Trans Canada Trail (Episode 51), said their review process takes up to 12 weeks. Other funders have told me that they have a clear window: 3 months from application to notification.

So don't panic if you don't hear right away; ask early in the process what the timeline looks like.

Understanding the Process

Once you've submitted a grant, it's out of your hands, but understanding what happens next can help you write smarter the next time. Funders shared what goes on behind the scenes, and it's clear that the review process is structured, thoughtful, and often more personal than you might expect.

What Happens After Submission

So, you've submitted the proposal. Now what? You wait, yes. But funders are busy behind the scenes.

What Happens Between Applying and Awarding

This is the part many people overlook, but it's full of opportunities, especially if you stay engaged and open to feedback.

Trans Canada Trail (Episode 51) reviews every piece of paperwork and often reaches out to applicants who are missing something. They don't want to disqualify; they want to help you finish strong.

In Episode 41, Magda Galindo, Director of Grants Management at FFAR, talked about what happens after you submit and why feedback matters so much: "If it passes administrative review, then all of our RFAs are peer reviewed by a group of three to five subject matter experts. And after that peer review takes place, then it moves over to an Advisory Council Review. And if it passes that review, then our Executive Director, Dr. Saharah Moon Chapotin, will sign off." It's a very rigorous process to get funded by FFAR.

Magda continued, "We tend to try to tell people what was lacking, so that in case they want to resubmit an application....for the most part, we do give comments back from our peer reviewers, so that even if they don't come back to FFAR, they know the general areas where they could potentially make changes and just improve the research they submitted."

This emphasis on feedback highlights a bigger truth from *GrantTalk* guests: grants aren't one-off transactions; they are opportunities to build lasting relationships that can lead to more support down the line.

That kind of review and notes can help you tweak things and come back stronger next time.

This is your reminder to stay reachable, stay responsive, and keep your phone nearby. You never know when that follow-up email will come. Use whatever information you receive in a rejection letter to modify and enhance your next proposal or to resubmit when the grant becomes available again.

One note of caution – if you did not apply for a grant and someone calls saying you did and need to pay taxes to receive it – stop talking and hang up – it is a fraudulent call.

This is why your grant calendar is so important to the process: it gives you something to look back at. Perhaps you applied two years ago, and they found some extra funds and really liked your proposal – you might accidentally hang up on them, too, thinking they are trying to scam you.

The Role of Relationships in Grant Funding

Grant funding isn't just about submitting applications; it is about building relationships. Many funders emphasize the importance of maintaining ongoing communication, attending funder-hosted workshops, and engaging in technical assistance sessions. Organizations that actively engage with funders beyond the application process are more likely to secure future funding (Episodes 10 and 18).

In Episode 18, Daniel McNeal, Director of the Quality of Life Grants Program, encourages applicants to seek feedback if their proposals are declined. Instead of seeing rejection as a failure, organizations should view it as an opportunity to improve. Many funders invite resubmissions, and they appreciate applicants who take their feedback seriously (Episode 10).

Relationships matter more than you might think. Traci Lanier from 10,000 Degrees (Episode 21) talked about how getting to know a funder, even informally, can lead to future support. One early "no" led to an advisory relationship that shaped future proposals and opened doors to new funders.

Brenda Swann (Episode 22) echoed this. Many of their repeat grantees are organizations that not only deliver good results but also stay in touch, attend funder meetings, and keep their programs visible in the community.

Submission and Review

Once you submit your proposal, it goes to the reviewers. These are real people, reading one application after another, trying to figure out who is ready and who isn't. Your job is to make their job easy.

Make It Easy for Reviewers to Say Yes

Laurel Meleski, Director of Operations at RedRover (Episode 27), said that the strongest applications clearly connect the dots: the problem, the plan, the people involved, and the funding needed.

Brenda Swann, the Director of Grants and Operations at the St. Johns County Cultural Council (Episode 22), echoed that well-structured proposals with aligned budgets and outcomes are easier to approve.

Every item in your proposal must be a line item in your budget, with the funding source identified.

Keep It Simple, But Strong

Reviewers aren't grading essays; they're making decisions. Samantha Walters, CEO and former Senior Strategist at Colocation

America (Episode 25), shared that her team reviews many applications, and the ones that are clear and concise always stand out.

The director of a foundation (Episode 29) reminded us that reviewers are busy. Keep your proposal focused, organized, and readable.

Building Relationships Beyond the Grant

Grants will open doors to more than just funding. In Episode 9, Kell Chole, Founder and Executive Director of the Institute of Traditional Irish Music, used a grant to launch a music education program and formed partnerships with schools, local artists, and sponsors.

At The Guest House Chicago (Episode 7), Adam Helman, Executive Director, shared how "We are a small nonprofit...and we've gotten a couple of very significant donations coming through GrantWatch, as well as some smaller foundations that have given us money year over year." (GrantWatch listed the grants that Adam Helman refers to.)

According to Adam Helman, "In my experience at GrantWatch, these networks are especially valuable for beginners, who can learn a great deal by starting small and building up."

Advice for First-Time Applicants

For those new to grant seeking, funders recommend starting with smaller grants to establish a track record. Demonstrating successful project management at a small-scale builds credibility and makes it easier to secure larger grants in the future (Episode 21).

Other key tips include ensuring proposals align with funder priorities, submitting complete and well-researched applications, and preparing financial documentation in advance. Funders also suggest that first-time applicants should reach out for guidance before submitting their applications, as many offer informational sessions or pre-application consultations (Episode 21).

Everyone starts somewhere. In Episode 6, Katy Sursa, Director of Development at United Cerebral Palsy of Arkansas, submitted a major transportation grant on a tight deadline, with support from her whole team. It was her first big win, and it gave her the confidence to apply again.

In Episode 3, Rosaline Bangura, Founder of Be Rose International Foundation, shared how she started grant writing during the Ebola crisis. With no formal training, she figured it out as she went and emphasized the importance of starting small and staying persistent.

Beyond these basics, one piece of advice that stands out from the *GrantTalk* interviews is to weave strong community ties into your application. Funders love seeing real involvement.

The Importance of Community Engagement

Funders prioritize projects that demonstrate strong community involvement. Applications that include letters of support from local stakeholders, partnerships with other organizations, or evidence of grassroots engagement often stand out in the selection process. Some funders even require applicants to present their proposals in community forums before final approval (Episodes 14 and 20).

Community-driven initiatives tend to have a stronger impact and greater sustainability. Funders look for projects that not only serve a community but also actively involve them in shaping solutions. Organizations that engage with the people they serve, listen to their needs, and build collaborative programs have a competitive advantage (Episodes 14 and 20).

This focus on collaboration reminds me of how empowering it is to bring young people into the process, as I've seen in episodes where teens lead their own grant-funded initiatives.

Training the Next Generation of Grant Writers

One of the things I loved most was hearing how young people are stepping into grant writing early.

Youth Service America (Episode 20) helps teens design and apply for their own service grants. It's powerful to see students leading hunger relief projects, reading initiatives, and neighborhood cleanups, funded through applications they submitted themselves.

This work isn't just about writing; it's about leadership. So, if you're mentoring others, show them how to read guidelines, write a basic budget, and tell their story. Let them co-author. Let them submit. Let them learn by doing, because the future of grant writing is already here; it just needs a little guidance.

As we train the next wave of grant writers and nonprofit leaders, it's also crucial to show how effective programs don't stand alone. We need to teach how they integrate into existing systems and collaborate [apply together] for greater impact.

Working Within Systems

Good programs know how to fit into the larger system around them. Laurel Meleski, Director of Operations at RedRover (Episode 27), explained how their Safe Housing grant works in coordination with domestic violence shelters and animal welfare groups. Their process requires applicants to already be working within shelter systems, because that's what keeps survivors and their pets safe. Strong proposals usually don't start from scratch; they build on existing work.

Mentorship Is Part of the Grant

When you get a grant, you're not just getting dollars, you're getting access. And often, that access means mentorship.

Soon Hagerty (Episode 52) doesn't just fund women entrepreneurs, she pairs them with a circle of five advisors for a full year. They cover finance, leadership, branding, manufacturing, and scaling. That kind of support is priceless.

Many funders, such as NMF, the Nonprofit Management Fund featured in Episode 48, also offer grant-writing cohorts. In fields with high request volumes, they are also experimenting with cohort models that allow larger groups to work with either shared or individual consultants before applying for the grant.

Years ago, when I wrote grants for NY State and NYC government agencies, in-person Q&A meetings were extremely helpful. To prepare for the review and the question-and-answer sessions, I would read the application and all its appendices and place sticky notes with my questions. After the session, they would post the

Q&A online and sometimes offer a clearer answer than what was presented at the workshop or add a new appendix to the application.

Forgive my metaphors, but if your grant funder offers a pathway to coaching, a webinar, or a workshop, walk through it. Do not leave vital information on the table; absorb it and use it.

Advice for Grant Writers

One question I always ask funders and recipients is: What advice would you give to a new grant writer? The answers were both honest and encouraging.

Ainsley Munro (Episode 51), Coordinator of Trail Infrastructure and Funding at Trans Canada Trail , told applicants not to give up, because great ideas will eventually find a home. Katy Sursa (Episode 6) said her first big win came from trusting herself and asking for help. And in Episode 3, Rosaline Bangura reminded us that you don't have to be trained, you just have to start.

If there's one thing all the funders agree on, it's this: you won't get funded if you don't apply. So read the directions, start writing, and ask questions along the way. You've got this.

Once you've landed that first grant, think bigger. Think about multi-year funding, where funders look for proven track records and long-term vision, as shared in several *GrantTalk* episodes.

What Funders Look for in a Multi-Year Funding Application

Multi-year funding is typically awarded to projects with a strong track record, a well-defined sustainability plan, and clear impact metrics. Funders are more likely to invest in organizations that have demonstrated success in previous grant cycles and have a clear plan to scale their impact over time (Episodes 9 and 21).

Long-term funding is also tied to an organization's ability to adapt and respond to challenges. Funders want to see that grantees can navigate obstacles and adjust their approach while maintaining progress toward their goals. A flexible, forward-thinking approach makes organizations more attractive candidates for multi-year support (Episodes 9 and 21).

When applying for renewed or extended funding, show your growth. In Episode 11, Robynn Takayama, Grants Manager, Community Challenge Grants, said they look for clear reporting, consistency, and signs of progress.

In Episode 12, George Vaughn, the Founder and Executive Director of StreeHeat-Ministries, Inc., a nonprofit, explained how his organization transitioned from a pilot project to a multi-year grant by demonstrating successful outcomes and strong community partnerships. If you want to keep the support coming, show what you've built.

From First Grant to Long-Term Partnership

Some grants are one-and-done. Others are the start of something bigger. Knowing which kind you're applying for can shape how you approach it.

Sometimes funders will invest in you for three- to five-year grants. But those awards depend on program compliance and ongoing communication.

If a funder is willing to invest in you for multiple years, they're expecting a partnership, not just paperwork. So, show them you're not just ready for the money, you're ready for the relationship.

Say Thank You, and Keep in Touch

One thing funders mentioned again and again? They don't hear "thank you" nearly enough.

It sounds small, but a thank-you note, a photo of your program, or a quick update goes a long way. It reminds funders why they believed in you in the first place and keeps you top of mind for the next cycle.

Lisa-Marie Haygood, Executive Director of the Cherokee County Educational Foundation (Episode 30), said she loves it when past grantees check in. So, say thank you. Send a follow-up. Build the relationship now, before you need to reapply.

These ongoing connections often highlight the most memorable projects funders have supported, which is why I asked several *GrantTalk* guests about the ones that stood out to them.

Stand Out Grant Funded Projects

In a few interviews, we asked which funded project stood out. I want to share these projects to illustrate the diversity of grant-funded initiatives, from environmental restoration to healthcare, education, and technology, each demonstrating how targeted funding can drive real, measurable impact.

The Community Rain Garden Project discussed in Episode 16 was simple yet highly effective. A rain garden was created at the Sanderlin Community Center in South St. Pete, Florida. This project, managed by the League of Women Voters, transformed a neglected drainage ditch into a thriving rain garden that filters stormwater before it reaches Tampa Bay. The project engaged the community center's diverse visitors and even included an educational component for schoolchildren. The kids participated in a scavenger hunt, learning about local plant species and pollinators while understanding how stormwater runoff affects water quality. This project was praised for its ability to engage the community while providing an environmental benefit, making it a replicable model for other areas looking to improve stormwater management

Wildlife Camera Citizen Science Project, also discussed in Episode 16, is another standout project conducted by Eckerd College in Tampa Bay. They deployed wildlife cameras at Fort De Soto Park to monitor local species and engaged the public through an interactive QR code system. Visitors could scan the code, view images captured by the cameras, and contribute their own observations. The project included a digital component in which students learned to code and to develop websites to display the collected data. This initiative blended environmental conservation, community engagement, and STEM education, making it an innovative and scalable approach to citizen science.

The Mobile Mammography Unit discussed in Episode 13 was a large-scale grant that enabled University Hospital to launch a mobile unit, ensuring underserved women had access to early breast cancer detection. This project, funded through a $500,000 grant, aimed to bring preventative healthcare directly to communities where women often lack transportation or financial resources to access routine screenings. Another $1 million grant was allocated to improve MRI services, demonstrating the significant impact of targeted healthcare funding in saving lives.

The **Hershey Heartwarming Hero Grant** was discussed in Episode 20. It was a small but mighty $500 grant from the Hershey Heartwarming Hero Fund that sparked a powerful peer-to-peer reading initiative. The project was designed to provide children with books through a buddy reading program. When the COVID-19 pandemic forced schools into lockdown, the program quickly pivoted to virtual reading sessions via Zoom. What started as a reading initiative evolved into a broader support system, with students providing homework help and social connection. This project demonstrated how even a small grant can have a lasting impact when paired with creativity and adaptability.

STEM Education and Telescopes discussed in Episode 30 was a grant program supporting STEM education, providing classroom impact grants of up to $2,500 to rural schools in Georgia, allowing students to study astronomy: the stars and planets, despite limited internet access. By providing web-based data packs and mobile hotspots, the program enabled students to engage in astronomy research without geographic limitations.

Other grants in this category supported 3D printers and music education, ensuring that students in underfunded schools had access to cutting-edge learning tools.

These stories show what is possible with the right funding. But some projects stick with you longer than others. They stay in your mind because they touch lives in big ways across different areas.

In Episode 16, Jessica Lewis, Community Projects Manager of the Tampa Bay Estuary Program, shared how their grant combined environmental science with public education and local arts. That kind of cross-sector impact grabs attention.

In Episode 15, Jen Swan-Kilpatrick, Executive Director & Holly Grant, Grants and Programming Director at Arts Services Inc. of Western New York in Buffalo, used funding to connect youth with professional artists and secure business sponsorships. A great project tells a great story.

Grants Are for Artists Too

Artists often think grants aren't for them, but they are. Alexis Hyde, Director of Art and Outreach at Quinn Emanuel Urquhart & Sullivan, LLP (Episode 40), shared how the firm of trial lawyers funds visual artists to work in its offices through its artists-in-residence program. It's not about charity; it's about recognizing the value of creativity.

There are plenty of grants that support artists, residencies, and arts education.

Artists get help from more than just foundations. Many businesses step in, too. They have found a simple way to fund artists that helps everyone.

I love this model. At GrantWatch, we see every day how arts grants help the whole community. They create jobs. They bring people together. They build stronger towns and cities.

Businesses Funding Artists: A Simple Model That Works

As Alexis Hyde shared in Episode 40, their program began during the COVID quarantine to help artists keep creating. "It was born out of quarantine... we've been talking about, what's the status of artists, like, how are they supporting themselves? What's going on? How difficult it is if they can't have art shows or studio visits. So, we came up with this idea: what if we put them here in the office? And we wanted to make sure it was something they could do and support themselves with. Because [being an] artist [is a] job, just like being a lawyer."

Alexis Hyde continued, "And so we came up with a nice number: $20,000 over four months to have an artist come in and use the office as a studio. And we had two artists in LA at a time. We do it twice a year here in LA, and we expanded to New York last year. I also have two artists in London, and it's all for local artists. So, it's the community that supports the firm's local office. So in LA, we have LA artists in New York, we have New York artists in London, we have London art based artists, and they just commute to work, just like the lawyers do, just like the associates do, and they come in and they work, and then at the end, we put on an exhibition and acquire a piece for the collection as well."

It's a simple way for businesses to give artists real support, and it shows how grants can pop up in unexpected places like law offices, turning empty office space into artist studios with a solid stipend, which can make a big difference. It's easy for other businesses to copy, gives local artists real support, and makes the workplace more enjoyable for everyone.

Grants Support Economic Growth and Community

Grants do more than just fund projects; they build community infrastructure. Traci Lanier from 10,000 Degrees (Episode 21) talked about how grant funding for college access programs is an investment in the local economy. In Episode 30, Lisa-Marie Haygood, Executive Director of the Cherokee County Educational Foundation, shared how teacher mini-grants support student success while also increasing teacher satisfaction and retention. These grants aren't just helpful, they're transformational.

You see the same big change in other areas, too. Food and agriculture are great examples. FFAR, as in Episode 41, supports research that advances food and agriculture science to develop tools, technologies, and information that benefit farmers, consumers, and the environment.

Grants for Food and Agriculture Research

Places like FFAR make it easier to fund big ideas in food and farming by partnering with others. Start with a quick LOI, get expert feedback, and don't hesitate to ask for help if you're not sure.

I always advise people to ask questions.

Music and Arts for Systemic Change and Well-Being.

Sarah Lyding, Executive Director of The Music Man Foundation (Episode 36), highlights how music-focused grants can address holistic needs, create transformative change, and foster lasting impact.

Sarah explained it this way, "Our mission is to amplify work that centers music to create enduring change... music is a force for good.

Music is a force for transformation... We know it promotes academic achievement among students. We know that there are cognitive breakthroughs for Alzheimer's patients. We know how impactful it can be for veterans returning from combat with their healing."

Foundations like The Music Man demonstrate how music-focused grants can create lasting transformations in education, veteran healing, and policy, encouraging applicants to embed the arts into core systems for enduring results.

Real change happens when people work together. That is why I love seeing businesses and nonprofits team up. They bring different strengths and make bigger things happen.

Innovative Local Funding Models: Lodging Taxes for Tourism and Infrastructure

Communities are finding new ways to create grants, too. Some use local taxes to fund projects that grow tourism and jobs. Just as local taxes build physical infrastructure, arts and music grants can create systemic change in education, health, and beyond.

Music and arts grants do that. They improve schools. They help health. They change lives for the better.

As Nan Devlin, Consultant and Grant Manager at Rural Tourism Partners, and former Executive Director of the Tillamook Coast Visitors Association, shared in Episode 33, innovative local taxes can create sustainable funding for community growth.

According to Nan Devlin, "There's this lodging tax we can implement that could bring in some dollars, some big dollars. And so they turned to our state and our state travel organization to help set up a lodging tax of 10%. There is a law ...set in 2003 by the state that said any new lodging tax implemented after 2003 had to go under a 70/30 split, and the 30% could go to anything the municipality wanted. In our case, it went toward helping repair roads... sustainable tourism. That's economic development."

Seventy percent of the 70/30 split of the lodging tax was returned to the community for arts, culture, and tourism.

This model demonstrates how grants from local revenue can drive economic development and tourism infrastructure.

Communities like Tillamook County (Episode 33) show how targeted taxes can fund signage, facilities, and marketing, benefiting both visitors and residents while fostering sustainable development.

Businesses and Nonprofits: Stronger Together

When a grant is available to either a business or a nonprofit, and both bring value, it's smart to choose the organization with the most compatible structure to lead. If both are eligible, go with the one that has the clearest track record, the strongest infrastructure, and the one that checks the right boxes for the funder's goals.

Some of the most innovative programs come from partnerships between nonprofits and businesses. Elliot Rosenfeld, President and CEO of Net Is Up and a cybersecurity expert (Episode 17), partners with nonprofits to deliver tech education and security training.

Funders love seeing collaborations, especially when collaborations strengthen both sides.

Ainsley Munro and Heidi Tillmanns at Trans Canada Trail (Episode 51) support projects that link municipalities, schools, and small businesses.

Brenda Swann (Episode 22) sees stronger proposals when they're backed by local partnerships.

In Episode 40, Alexis Hyde talked about how these artist programs do more than just help artists; they make the whole office a better place. "The lawyers, the associates, the administrative staff here get to see the artist's job. They see the artists come in five days a week and work. You know that it's not just like a hobby after work, having a glass of wine and a little painting, that it's, it's what's real work...It's such a treat...it will absolutely raise your staff's morale, because they feel great that they're included in an art thing... You do get a new appreciation for how art is made."

When people see artists at work every day, it changes how they think about art and boosts everyone's spirits. It's a win for the community, too. I would be thrilled to talk to working artists every day.

Collaboration tells a story, and funders are always looking for those rooted in community.

Are There Grants for Businesses?

Yes, absolutely, businesses, especially those driving social impact, are showing up strong in the grant world. Whether you're focused on workforce development, digital transformation, or teaming up with nonprofits to serve your community, there's money on the table.

The key? Be strategic. Know what you're offering, how it creates value beyond profit, and align it with funders who care about impact.

Grants aren't just for nonprofits anymore; they're for businesses that move with purpose. We saw that change dramatically with COVID, when all of a sudden, many more grants became available for businesses.

Lisa Evangelos, National Administrator of the Culinary Federation, in Episode 35, reminded us, "the hospitality industry was very struck by COVID... not being able to operate... So, we were looking for creative ways to bring in revenue... that's how I was introduced to Grant Watch."

Economic growth is of utmost importance to the country, the state or province, and the local community. Economic growth is achieved by lowering business costs and increasing employment.

On GrantWatch, we research grants for nonprofits, individuals, and businesses. We have listed grants for research and development, job creation, infrastructure improvements, startup grants, business expansion, incentives to encourage businesses to relocate to certain locations, community development, neighborhood revitalization, and the creation of new local jobs. We have 61 grant categories on GrantWatch, including grants for businesses.

You've made it through this chapter full of *GrantTalk* Secrets, and hopefully, you're already thinking about your first (or next) grant. Here's my final piece of advice in this chapter: write that first proposal. Don't wait for perfect timing or perfect wording. Just begin, and to help you, GrantWatch has created the AI GrantWatch Grant Writing Tool (see Chapter IV).

And when you finish writing your first grant? That's when you apply for your second.

Grant writing is a skill that builds over time. Like anything worth doing, it takes patience, persistence, and a little creativity. Use what you've learned here, learn from others, and trust your mission.

The world needs what you're building. And there's more ahead – how our staff reacted to and learned from a twenty-day platform challenge to help you do the same, how to grow your visibility, and how to use new tools wisely.

Our Podcast Guests

All the ideas in Chapter I came from real people who shared them on GrantTalk. Here is the full list of our first 52 guests. You can go back and listen to any episode for more details. Most job titles and organization names reflect those held at the time of filming. People may have been promoted or moved into new roles since then.

#	Title	Guest Name	Job Title	Organization
1	Transforming Lives at Williamson College of the Trades	Mary Jane Taylor	Director of Grants and Research	Williamson College of the Trades
2	From Grants to Great Performances, Inside Sequim City Band's Journey	David Proebstel	Treasurer	Sequim City Band
3	From Grants to Good Deeds - The Be Rose International Foundation Story	Rosaline Bangura	Founder	Be Rose International Foundation
4	Help Comes to Haiti and the Mississippi Delta with Nonprofit Grants	Dina Ray	Director of Development	But God Ministries
5	$800K in Urban Farming Grants to CBOs in 10 Cities from T.I.M.E.'s $12M Initiative	LaGrand & Eric Elliott	Founders	T.I.M.E. Inc.
6	Katy Sursa's Grant Journey at United Cerebral Palsy of Arkansas With GrantWatch	Katy Sursa	Director of Development	UCP United Cerebral Palsy of Arkansas
7	The Guest House Chicago - Tips for Nonprofit Management and Grant Writing	Adam Helman	Executive Director	The Guest House
8	Grants for Rehab of Children With Disabilities: CRIT TeletonUSA & Steven Silver	Steven Silver	Philanthropic Advisor Former Grants Manager	Philanthropic Services of the Southwest / Children's Rehabilitation Institute Teleton USA (CRIT USA)
9	How to Get a Grant for Children in Music, with Libby Hikind and Kell Chole	Kell Chole	Founder/ Executive Director and Grant Recipient	Institute of Traditional Irish Music
10	How Mercy Medical Free Clinics Found Success	Wayne Jackson	Executive Director	Mercy Medical Free Clinics

#	Title	Guest Name	Job Title	Organization
	with GrantWatch			
11	Secrets to Successful Grant Writing & Community Engagement | Robynn Takayama	Robynn Takayama	Grants Manager	Community Challenge Grants
12	Impacting Communities: StreeHeat-Ministries, Inc. Succeeds with GrantWatch	George Vaughn	Founder and Executive Director	StreeHeat-Ministries, Inc.
13	Connie Dwyer Breast Cancer Center: Supporting Women with Breast Cancer!	Sarah Roberts	Director	Connie Dwyer Breast Cancer Foundation
14	Bookmobile Grants & Sunshine Family Outreach Center	Bobbi Donovan	President and CEO, and Educator	Sunshine Family Outreach Center
15	Inspire Creativity with Arts Services Inc. and GrantWatch	Jen Swan-Kilpatrick & Holly Grant	Director & Grants Manager	Arts Services Inc. of Western New York
16	Environmental grants with the Tampa Bay Estuary Program	Jessica Lewis	Community Projects Manager	Tampa Bay Estuary Program
17	Cybersecurity Essentials for Small Businesses & Nonprofits with Elliot Rosenfeld	Elliot Rosenfeld	President and CEO	Net Is Up
18	Grant Tips, Superman, and The Christopher & Dana Reeve Foundation	Daniel McNeal	Director, Quality of Life Grants Program;	Christopher & Dana Reeve Foundation
19	Matt Berkowitz on PEOs and Their Benefits	Matthew Berkowitz	President and CEO	All Set PEO Consultants (formerly at G&A Partners)
20	Katie Reusch Explains the Youth Service America Grants for Youth	Katie Reusch	Director of Youth Programs	YSA, Youth Service America
21	10,000 Degrees Helps Low-Income Students Go to College	Traci Lanier	Vice President	10,000 Degrees
22	St Johns Cultural	Brenda	Director of Grants	St. Johns Cultural

#	Title	Guest Name	Job Title	Organization
	Council: Arts Grants for Artists, Nonprofits, and Businesses	Swann	and Operations	Council
23	Expert Grant Writing Tips from Grant Writer Helena Kosoff	Helena Kosoff	Grant Writer	Grant Writing Consultant
24	The Pilcrow Foundation Has Grants for Books for Rural Libraries and Disaster Relief	Karren Timmermans	President & Executive Director	The Pilcrow Foundation
25	Colocation America and K-12 STEM Innovation Grants	Samantha Walters	CEO, formerly Senior Strategist	Colocation America
26	Learn About Donor-Advised Funds and Grant Funding for Nonprofits with Karin Beyer	Karin Beyer	Director of Community Philanthropy	Otsego Community Foundation
27	Animal Rescue Grants and Pet Friendly Shelters from RedRover	Laurel Meleski	Laurel Meleski	Director of Operations	RedRover
28	Connect with an OWWLL Audio Call for Expert Business Networking	Jason R. Hill	Jason R. Hill	Founder	OWWLL
29	Grants and Scholarships for Sustainable Waste Management		Senior Director of Programs	
30	Cherokee County Educational Foundation Grants for Teachers	Lisa-Marie Haygood	Lisa-Marie Haygood	Executive Director	Cherokee County Educational Foundation
31	Grants Provide After-School Programs for The Wade Center	Karen Harvey	Karen Harvey	Grant Writer	Westminster at Wade (DBA Wade Center)
32	Strengthen Communities with United Way Funding	Jessica Safransky Schacht	Jessica Safransky Schacht	COO	United Way of Racine County
33	How Grants Empower Tourism at the Tillamook	Nan Devlin	Consultant and Grant Manager,	Rural Tourism Partners

#	Title	Guest Name	Job Title	Organization
	Coast Visitors Association | Nan Devlin		and former Executive Director	Tillamook Coast Visitors Association
34	Unlocking PR Power for Nonprofits & Businesses | Sandy Collier Hey, Sandy! PR	Sandy Collier	PR Professional	Hey, Sandy! PR & Communications
35	A Closer Look at the Grant Journey of Canada's Culinary Federation | Lisa Evangelos	Lisa Evangelos	National Administrator	Culinary Federation of Canada
36	Hitting The Right Note for Education with The Music Man Foundation | Sarah Lyding	Sarah Lyding	Executive Director	The Music Man Foundation
37	Can Grants Turn Failure into Innovation	Tim Tramble, Sr.	President & CEO	Saint Luke's Foundation
38	Grants For STEM Education and K-12 Students	Dr. Allison J. Hamilton Molnar	Executive Director	Citizens for Nuclear Technology Awareness
39	Applying for Community Foundation Grants	Ryanne Jennings	President & CEO	Wayne County Community Foundation
40	Artist-in-Residence Grants	Alexis Hyde	Director of Art and Outreach	Quinn Emanuel Urquhart & Sullivan, LLP (Trial Lawyers)
41	FFAR Is Fueling Innovation with Agricultural Grants	Magda Galindo	Director of Grants Management	FFAR, Foundation for Food & Agriculture Research
42	Digitization Grants Preserve History		Program Officer	A Library Foundation
43	The Community Fund of Ohio is Empowering the Disabled with Grants	Sharon McGraw, Ed.D	Grant Program Officer	Community Fund Ohio
44	From Combat to Compassion, Serving Vets with Grants	Homer Lee Bizzle III, M.A. Ed	President CEO	America Cares Too

#	Title	Guest Name	Job Title	Organization
45	FFP Connects Nonprofits with Pro Bono Certified Financial Planners (CFPs)	Rachel Roth	Senior Director of Grants & Programs	Foundation For Financial Planning
46	$200K in Grants for Arts and Science Immigrant Organizations		Grants Officer	
47	Building Ramps to Improve Life for Seniors and Veterans	Melanie Reeves	Executive Director	RiverLife
48	Grants That Strengthen Operations | The Nonprofit Management Fund	Eloiza Altoro	Fund Advisor	Nonprofit Management Fund
49	An Organization That Helps Artists | Huntington Arts Council	Patty Eljaiek	Long Island Grants for the Arts Coordinator	Huntington Arts Council
50	Grants to Protect Arctic Wildlife | World Wildlife Fund	Elisabeth Kruger	Manager of Arctic Wildlife	World Wildlife Fund
51	Unlock Trail Funding: Trans Canada Trail Grants Revealed!	Ainsley Munro, Heidi Tillmanns	Ainsley Munro, Coordinator of Trail Infrastructure and Funding, and Heidi Tillmans Director of Trail Infrastructure and Funding at Trans Canada Trail	Trans Canada Trail
52	Boundless Futures: Fueling Women Founders with Grit, Grants, and Guidance	Soon Hagerty	Co-Founder and President	Boundless Futures Foundation

11: Marketing and Visibility

This morning, I spoke with my staff. It is not the first time we have discussed marketing, and it will not be the last. I want to instill the idea that marketing is integral to everyone's role in the company.

Why? Because we all have different eyes, hearts, souls, and values, and what we produce as an organization needs to be welcoming and inviting to all.

GrantWatch aims to objectively inform, open new grant opportunities for the greater good, and motivate people to pursue grants to support and bring their initiatives to fruition.

Every employee at GrantWatch is also a marketer, or the new term "brand ambassador," through customer support and satisfaction, web development and design, blog articles, video creation, graphic design, social media, paid ads, and public speaking.

The team knows that, to succeed, the company needs to retain its current subscribers and attract new ones across all platforms. To increase revenue, "Everyone Needs to Know Our Company Name" in a positive way.

I sincerely believe that every piece of content produced by a nonprofit or business must sell its brand. If you are a business or nonprofit, your logo needs to pop! Your content needs to complement your brand.

Everything you write and express needs to be truthful and real. What you write must add value to the reader. Your product must meet quality standards and be high-quality.

Bait-and-switch is not a marketing tactic you want to employ. It is when an ad draws people in with one promise but gives them something different once they are already invested. Sometimes, even honest and above-board businesses are accused of bait-and-switch, so I tell my staff to make sure it is not a valid complaint about our marketing.

Brand Recognition and Trust

If you haven't yet named your nonprofit or company, choose a name that is also available as a website domain with the .com, and if applicable, also purchase the .org extension for that name.

Your organization's name becomes your brand, and it needs to mean something to you and represent your company, conveying your mission, vision, products, or goals.

Your name should be short, easy to say, and easy to remember. Three syllables should be the maximum if you want people to remember your name. Fifteen-character domains, or even fewer, will work best.

Not every business can have a one-word name, but if you can, name your business with six meaningful letters, with consistent marketing and color palette, and you will certainly be remembered.

People are more likely to support or engage with an organization they recognize and trust. Consistent use of your nonprofit or business name across all platforms (website, social media, marketing materials) strengthens brand recognition, making it easier for people to identify, remember, and distinguish your brand from competitors.

This advice is simplistic, but it's your name, and it represents your company, differentiates your brand, and makes it easier for customers to choose your products or services.

Start sketching your logo ideas and look at colors until you feel comfortable. You can use software, a contractor, or create it yourself.

I built my business with my gut. I had to like all designs, and there was no science involved. If artwork makes me nauseous or dizzy, I don't approve of it.

Something to warn you about, that I wish I had known and checked. Some logos must always be placed on a white background. The green in the Watch part of the GrantWatch logo sometimes causes us trouble. So, think about all the possibilities before you settle on your colors.

I hope to explain our journey and what worked for us. I want to teach you to use all the tools available for your business, nonprofit, or as an individual. It takes immense passion and energy to achieve positive notoriety and growth.

But let me warn you that I do not make decisions based purely on statistics. I throw it all at the wall, and I see what sticks. I will use numbers to measure growth, but my big-picture initiatives are not necessarily driven by them.

My staff can give me numbers, and I truly appreciate those meetings – hearing which words we are optimized for and how many people clicked through from an article to the website, but I look to the real bottom line: sign-ups, sales, and revenue. The truth is, we never really know how many times someone heard about us before they took an action. We can only "sometimes" know the immediate page they came from before they took an action, on that day.

Are you ready to hear about our marketing journey? Let's go!

Two Years After "The Queen of Grants"

What transpired since the publication of *The Queen of Grants: From Teacher to Grant Writer to CEO* is something I want to share with you.

Bear with me as I recount the tale of twists and turns that led to another great idea, and then to an even greater one.

Let me reminisce a bit about the time when my graphic artist, Jon Flor (may his soul rest in peace), who designed the original book cover for *The Queen of Grants,* was creating the artwork template for our testimonial social media posts.

Jon unilaterally decided to design a logo called 'GrantTalk' for the testimonial templates for social posts. The logo used the exact colors and font of GrantWatch. When I saw it, I said, "Definitely, not! I am not branding another logo and confusing it with GrantWatch."

As Jon would say, "We are not doing it because Libby put the kibosh on it!" I am like that: my gut drives most of my decisions, and perhaps that's why, when I am ill, it always starts there. (or as my kids would say, LOL).

However, as most artists don't like destroying their work, the logo was saved in our files.

In January 2024, we were making numerous revisions to the cover of *The Queen of Grants*. With all the hearts representing content, things were forever evolving as I went through edits.

There are so many requirements and details regarding the shape, size, and bleed lines that we had to upload new versions repeatedly until both Amazon and IngramSpark finally accepted the book covers.

Note to self: leave yourself a few days to upload your cover artwork when you plan your release date. I was confident that the last version was only a small text tweak, and I had looked at the cover ad nauseam after like 20 revisions, so I did not carefully review the proof before I hit publish. I uploaded it with a publishing date of February 1st, 2024.

In early February, Paula, my physical trainer who had gotten me through the recovery phase of my knee replacement surgery and had patiently listened to my meanderings, helping me through writer's block, was the first to purchase a copy of *The Queen of Grants* and ask me for my autograph.

She presented me with the first physical copy of my book that I had ever seen. While signing the book for her, it felt surreal to see my book in print. I was very much in awe. I signed it right there in the gym.

Author copies take a much longer time to arrive, so I had not seen mine. She took a video of me on my iPhone as I looked at the book, flipped the pages, and signed her copy. For me, it was a momentous occasion. I still did not notice anything amiss with the book cover.

As I was sharing the video on WhatsApp with Sue, whom I consider to be my "right hand", she pointed out that all was not well. Oh no! The logo at the bottom of the book said, "GrantTalk."

By then books had already been sold.

I quickly bought the domain, GrantTalk.com, just in case anyone got any ideas, and we corrected the error by uploading yet another revised book cover with the GrantWatch logo.

We had to wait 72 hours for the new file upload to be approved and available. Until then, anyone who purchased the book had a cover featuring GrantTalk. I wonder today who, besides Paula, has a book with the GrantTalk logo.

Soon after my book was published, I was a guest in-studio on the OWWLL Podcast, filmed in a small studio within an office (they have since expanded to much larger digs). I think that, both before and after the interview, the seed of my very own podcast, *GrantTalk*, started to grow. A mistake became an opportunity.

A very short time later, I was rocking. I had a website; I wrote a book. I was called the Queen of Grants, and I had my own podcast, interviewing grant recipients and the foundations that awarded them.

It all came together with the publication of my book, and Sandy of Hey, Sandy! PR & Communications was ready to represent me.

Sandy, forever needed to know who won a grant on GrantWatch to sell me to local and not-so-local TV stations – so we already had a list for prospective podcast guests,

Hey, Sandy! PR & Communications is the PR company I wrote about in my last book. After my book was published, they sent me on a book tour, and I traveled across the USA to promote my first book, *The Queen of Grants,* the website GrantWatch.com, and the *GrantTalk* podcast.

I've appeared on the television shows *Lifestyle Today* and *Liftoff with Jeanniey Walden* in New York City; *Good Morning Washington* WJLA in Washington, D.C.; WTVC ABC's The Daily Refresh in Chattanooga, Tennessee; and *WPTV ABC* in West Palm Beach, Florida.

While the plan was for me to continue traveling and I was fully booked, my husband wasn't feeling well, so, as grounded as I was, I did live and pre-recorded TV and podcast interviews, with appearances across the United States. I believe they are currently on the Media pages of GrantWatch and on our YouTube channel (please subscribe to the free channel. All our GrantTalk episodes are there, too).

I was interviewed by TV stations in Tulsa, Oklahoma; Columbia, South Carolina; WICS ABC in Springfield, Illinois; Lexington, Kentucky; on Marketplace; Dayton, Ohio; Salt Lake City, Utah; Little Rock, Arkansas; and finally in Baltimore, Maryland.

Having learned how to publish a book, I already had the idea for this one gelling. I realized I wanted to write about what I learned from all the interviews, share the results of all the podcasts, and so much more, so I started writing this book. In my home, we call it Queen 2.

I need to tell you that every writer knows about distractions. Well, mine was quite positive because, intertwined with working on *The Queen of Grants 2*, I became a children's book author.

Over the past year, I have published 8 beautiful children's books with accompanying coloring books:

- Bailey Bullied Me: and I Am Kinder Now

- Fifty Stars Go Back to School: The Cheat Sheet That Became the Study Guide

- Mr. Squirrel's Spring Cleaning Lesson: A Tale of Tidiness and Teamwork

- Rikki Wants A Pet: How a Fluttery Surprise Saved the Day

- Twig Literacy: A Fun Story About Beavers, Money (Twigs), and Saving

- Why Won't You Fly, Sky?: A Tale of Finding the Courage to Soar

- Why Won't You Go to School, Kiki Kangaroo?: How Everyone Helped Him: School Is Scary - Until It's Not

- Ziva the Zebra Runs Away: A Story About the Beauty of Being Yourself

One day, I was not focused and a bit disillusioned because I did not see the endgame of Queen 2. The book wasn't cohesive, and My Table of Contents was all over the place. I found myself with my feet up on the couch, scrolling through X, and all these motivational videos started popping up.

I want to publicly thank the X algorithm. Videos that were once filmed in black and white were resurrected and reposted by accounts like @LeadersJunction, focusing on intention, manifestation, and making things happen.

There were a lot of voices from the past suddenly everywhere, reminding me of things I already knew but wasn't practicing. They kept showing up, and eventually I stopped scrolling and started listening to intentions, manifesting my goals, and making things happen.

I opened the manuscript file for Queen 2 and reread what I had already written. To inch forward, I began using affirmations, creating vision boards, and writing long-term and short-term goals.

I realized how engrossed I was when the winter holidays arrived. It was past time to look on Amazon for a unique gift for my staff. I already knew what was helping me, and I couldn't imagine any smiles from what was available that everyone would love.

I started creating a planner journal book for them (with Adrian and Ariel sworn to secrecy), using everything that was now working for me. Adrian helped me design the cover, and Ariel and I were counting the number of journaling pages needed for each month. I added the GrantWatch logo, and Sue sent the journals out to my staff across the globe. They arrived in mid-January, and I was a bit late as usual.

It turned out so well that we released it to the public in January 2026. *Organizing My Thoughts, Manifesting My Goals 2026: A Journal for Reflection, Planning, and Achievement,* a 500-page book, is complete with vision boards and monthly and weekly goals and has been incredibly well received.

I can already envision retailers asking for it next year when I make the 2027 version. The journal is available on libbyhikind.com, Amazon, and major online retailers in both color and in black-and-white for a slightly lower cost.

While it was yet another distraction from completing this book by my self-imposed February 1, 2026, deadline (which I did not exactly meet – it took a few more days than that), it turned out to be a very helpful tool to get my mojo back and running.

I am taking a bow, patting myself on the back, and already planning what comes next.

And don't you know it - that while revising the cover for this book, I worked on the cover to Queen 3. I will forever be young, as we changed the colors of my outfit to match the new cover design. I wasn't ready to give up the cover Jon designed, so I decided to make a trilogy of covers and keep his memory vibrant.

The Queen of Grants 3 will speak about writing children's books and whatever else I get myself into over the next few months or years.

But I digress. Let me begin with my marketing motto for the past twenty-five years: "Throw it all at the wall and see what sticks."

And why do I continuously say that? At GrantWatch, we want to build brand recognition and trust. We want to build it, rebuild it, and live inside it. We never really know what will bring that recognition or how someone will find us. Marketing venues and software have dramatically changed since 2010, when we started. Will we be successful through a podcast, one of my books, social media, Google ads, Facebook ads, or television? Will it come from a press release, a post about a live event, a personal meeting, or the slow and steady work of developing and mining our email lists?

The answer is yes to all. Videos that promise you can get rich if you do this or that are wrong because there is no single method to success. It is pushing through all the barriers with all the methods.

There is no single marketing technique, no single winning method, that magically grows a business. Growth comes from (G-d first), from visibility, and visibility comes from doing it all. Think of My Fair

Lady, "With a little bit of luck..." You throw it all at the wall, not hoping for anything to stick, but trusting that many things will.

Everyone Needs to Know Your Name

When people know your name positively, it directly drives growth and impacts your nonprofit or business's brand, customer trust, and overall market presence. When people know your name, you will have a greater ability to build credibility, increase visibility, achieve your mission and goals, and make a meaningful impact in the world.

When everyone knows your name, you will attract supporters, volunteers, employees, interns, and customers. It enhances your ability to advocate for change and supports your organization's long-term sustainability.

Ensuring your nonprofit's name is well known should be a key component of your branding and outreach strategy.

The principles of marketing for nonprofits and businesses share many similarities. Here are several strategies and tactics to help you successfully market your nonprofit or business.

You should begin with strategies that you are most comfortable with and engage with your staff and contractors to support their implementation.

To grow your business or nonprofit, you need to market. That is how everyone will know your name, understand who you are, and use your product or services. I am a "throw everything at the wall and see what sticks" strategist. At GrantWatch, we do it all and are still looking for new and innovative marketing ideas.

We can maintain low subscription costs by marketing and attracting new subscribers. I am going to share my knowledge to date, and hope it helps your business reach the point where everyone knows your name.

Social Media Marketing, Showing Up

Today, there are many social media platforms. Many more than when we started the company in 2010. When you first begin, set up social accounts on all platforms to reserve the name of your nonprofit or business. Save the user and password information and build the one or two you want to focus on.

Once you feel you have conquered those two, you will want to increase your reach.

On one of my sleepless nights, while playing around on X, I noticed that a very large account had followed me. I followed them back and sent a message.

"I am working on another book. Question: What is your strategy to obtain so many followers?"

I need to tell you that I was shocked. Growth Hackers, whose CEO is Jonathan Aufray and has 170.4K followers, responded to me within a minute.

"Hi Libby, Nice to hear about your upcoming book. To get followers, you want a mix of:

• Publishing different types of posts (e.g., text posts, threads, and videos)

• Retweeting others

• Commenting and answering comments

• Following people in your industry

Hope this helps,

Matt" (Matthew Davis)

Through a few more texts, I found out that about 6 high-level staff members have access to their X account, and they spend cumulatively about 1 to 2 hours a day on X. They agree with me that politics is the #1 topic on X, but Tech, AI Automation, and Web3 come in second.

That should give my staff and you a heads-up on what content will draw attention to your brand if you can spin it that way. Your social media posts need to be useful and targeted to your audience. Each social media site has a different main audience.

The main social sites for the average professional who is not interested in nefarious conspiracy theories or hyper-right or hyper-left content are currently Facebook, YouTube, Instagram, LinkedIn, and X. These are the most effective.

Over the years, my social media team has taught me the importance of a daily social media calendar that covers all channels and themes. Over time, we've moved from a Google Doc to Asana, and now to a hybrid approach. Asana helps us manage images from graphic designers, and the Google Doc gives us space to plan day-to-day for blog titles, holidays, and themes.

Just the other day, I added a posting responsibility chart. While we've established a great workflow for who writes what, who creates the images, and who edits, I noticed some channels weren't receiving posts that had already been prepared. Now, if I see a day missed, I know who dropped the ball. And if someone is out sick, someone else needs to pick up the slack.

Why is this so important? Because building a social media presence means you don't get to post once and call it a week. You have to keep showing up. I've seen articles go viral with 50,000+ views, but that doesn't happen every day. You can't sit around waiting for that GOAT article, the greatest of all time. You have to keep doing your best, take what is trending, and see if it can be used in your post to relate to what you are marketing; if not, become a trendsetter.

You post. Then you post again. You share. You join groups. You like other people's content. You comment, and not just "great post," but comments that lead people back to you. This is networking.

The commenting, liking, and sharing are the same thing you would do at a conference during a meet-and-greet, except now you're doing it online, in real time, every day.

I had thought it would be neat to become a TikTok influencer, but I realized that, at this point, it is "not" my goal in life to put on makeup and a new outfit every single day to post on TikTok. The camera loves younger people a whole lot more than me. They show up in a T-shirt and jeans and look great. Me? I can handle photo shoots about once a week, at most.

My new team lead (see Chapter 4) has thankfully taken over short video marketing for now. The long form is done by our videographer. We use all the new software, testing one product after another to get our message out.

My PR people strongly disagree and want me in front of the camera much more often, so we will see what I will do after I publish this book.

Content Built to Last

You know what you want to write, but will anyone want to read it? How can you be sure that your content will be read? There are several ways to identify what is trending in your area.

Start by identifying current issues, challenges, and interests within the nonprofit or business sector.

What you put on the internet stays there forever. That is why the smartest approach is to create evergreen content. Advice and guidance should remain helpful and relevant no matter the year or season.

In our *GrantNews* newsletter, we regularly feature real grants that come with specific deadlines. We can include time-sensitive items because we always surround them with timeless elements. Practical tips, clear step-by-step guidance, real stories from nonprofit professionals, and actionable advice that anyone can use long-term to make a difference.

Readers keep returning to reading those core pieces even after a grant opportunity has passed.

The same principle powers our three blogs. *GrantNews* delivers current grant news and insights. *GrantTalk* shares open conversations with people working in the grant space every day. *GrantWriterTeam* provides straightforward, hands-on advice for writing stronger proposals and building effective teams. All three thrive when the focus stays on lasting value that truly helps nonprofit folks in their daily work.

I always tell my team, "When you are writing articles for *GrantNews*, *GrantTalk*, or *GrantWriterTeam*, lean toward topics that hold up over time. Think about the challenges your readers face year after year. Crafting winning grant proposals, building and keeping loyal donors, or maintaining strong volunteer engagement and motivation are reliable evergreen pain points."

Titles play a big role in making that content discoverable and clickable for years to come. Start by identifying the main keywords people actually type into search engines. Tools like Google Keyword Planner and SEMrush are great for spotting them. Layer in more specific long-tail keywords to attract a targeted audience. Add a few powerful words to spark interest, address the pain point head-on, and keep everything concise and clear.

That simple formula produces strong, long-lasting titles like "The Ultimate Guide to Grant Writing Success" or "7 Strategies to Keep

Volunteers Coming Back." They draw readers in today and continue to perform well months or years later.

Once the article is live, take a moment to track its performance. Look at which topics and titles resonate most with your audience through views, time on page, shares, or comments. Use those real insights to shape what you create next. It is one of the best ways to keep improving.

Finally, if an older article feels dated or less accurate, resist the urge to delete it. Instead, set up a proper forwarding link to a newer, related piece. People bookmark, share, and find those older links all the time. Dead links harm your SEO, and there is no good reason to discard content that can still provide value.

Keeping good material alive and redirected builds trust with readers and search engines alike. It is a small habit that makes a big difference in keeping your sites strong and useful over the long run.

Healthy Email Lists

Building an email list is essential for any business, and you need to own your list. I learned that lesson the hard way.

Back in 2010, when we started the website, the email provider where I kept my entire subscriber list kicked me off their platform. I was getting too many spam reports and unsubscribes. We had a one-time free offer for 24 hours of website access, and people were signing up using fake email addresses to get it.

To the email provider, it was a small list. To me, it was everything. Because it was a small list, the percentage of bad email addresses was too high, and just like that, I was out.

Remember, people sign up all the time using fake or throwaway email addresses. The technology at the time was not as sophisticated as it is today.

As a company, you have to decide whether to require a verification process before people receive your emails, or whether your list is large enough that you can simply add them and let bad addresses fall off naturally over time. There's no one right answer. It depends on your volume, your goals, and how much risk you are willing to carry.

Moments like that teach you fast. We built our own CRM so we would never lose our list again, with access limited to company insiders only. Lesson learned.

Today, there are great tools that let you use an API on your website to send what I call transactional emails. That means you can tailor messages to your audience, rather than blasting the same thing to everyone and hoping for the best.

After every email launch, I suggest you check your stats early. Look at opens, unique clicks, and total clicks because they tell different stories. Are people opening emails? Are they clicking through to the website? Are they stopping there, or moving deeper? Those answers will tell you whether the message resonates or needs to be rewritten. Sometimes you will just need to tweak the subject line. Sometimes you'll need to change your image. If you check your email inbox, you may see replies telling you to scrap the marketing email and try again. That's part of the process.

And let's talk about list health, because this part matters. Email lists need to be cleaned often. People change jobs. They abandon inboxes. They stop caring. Holding on to dead emails does no one any good and can even hurt your deliverability. I'd rather have a smaller, healthier list than a bloated one with a poor open rate.

Email is still one of the most effective marketing tools. Once your email enters an inbox, someone will eventually see your subject line and header. Maybe they open it. Maybe they don't. Maybe they open the third one instead of the first. That's fine. This is the "throw everything at the wall" approach in action. You keep showing up, you keep refining, and over time, visibility compounds. Eventually, something sticks.

I have to tell you that we have had people receive GrantWatch emails for ten years, and then, one day, they decide to pay for a subscription. There is no rhyme or reason to it. I can't get inside their heads, but clearly something shifted. Maybe a new job suddenly required them to look for grants. Maybe they finally stopped procrastinating. Maybe their nonprofit realized that their federal funding was drying up and they needed a new revenue stream.

I did not consider those emails dead weight because the email owner was periodically opening them. They stayed connected, and when the moment was right, they acted.

If I had removed those people from our list, they would never have received our weekly grant emails or converted to becoming paid subscribers.

Create New Email Content

I do love those few seconds when I see a person's eyes light up when I am introduced, when they connect the dots between my name and GrantWatch, and when I am told how many people were helped by a grant we listed.

We run three blogs, *GrantNews*, *GrantWriterTeam*, and *GrantTalk*, and we always have new, relevant content to share with our subscribers.

In August 2024, I was standing in a long, slow line at a tourist shop in Alaska, chatting with the young woman behind me. You know the social drill. What do you do for work? Where are you from? Which ship are you on? It turned out she was on my ship. We exchanged business cards, the way people do, and when she looked at me, she lit up. She worked for a nonprofit and read our blog every day. She loved our emails.

The impromptu video from that moment can be found on the Media tab in the navigation bar, under the On the Road with GrantWatch dropdown. I'm there in a sun hat, visiting Alaska from Florida, standing next to Lara Cochran, who was working at the time for the Boys Hope Girls Hope organization in New York. Behind us are fully taxidermized animals, frozen in place, silently witnessing one of the most unlikely networking moments of my life.

Writers have no idea about the reach of their words in a blog article. I was quite surprised by this serendipitous meeting.

That moment still makes me smile because she felt like she already knew me. Not because we had met before, but because of the visibility our marketing emails created. She read them. She trusted them. And there we were, in Alaska, proof that showing up consistently works, even when you least expect it.

And that's what marketing is really all about. Give quality, and people become your readers. If they are your readers, they will be interested in what you have to offer.

Public Speaking Questions to Ask in Advance

I want to tell you that when you sign up to speak at an event, you need to decide what your time is worth. Your staff gets involved in preparing, writing a press release, helping with PowerPoint, even to refresh it, and then travel time, a make-up artist, and hey, you want to memorialize it for your website, so you might take a photographer with you. I learned the hard way that, for the most part, free events are a waste of my time.

If I sound a little sour, it's because of something that happened recently. I only found out how few people had signed up as the event date approached. When I give my word, I keep it, but in retrospect, I should have cancelled.

My young adult grandkids were visiting (I did not know that when I accepted the date), and I dragged them along. It was embarrassing, as it also rained, so there were even fewer than I was told. I spoke as if the room was packed, and it was filmed.

However, aside from family, I am still embarrassed to say there were 11 people there. Maybe I will watch the video after I publish this book and work with the videographer, so more people can hear me speak. I hope my grandkids learned that I keep my word, am gracious, even when I have a letdown. I spoke as if the entire auditorium was full.

Live Events, Bring New Business Energy

When I speak at conferences where people have paid to attend, I find myself in a large room full of people, and I am in my element. The following day, I am psyched about new ideas after hearing from people what they wanted and needed on my website.

Having a ticket price for an event is important. In my previous story, it was a free event as part of an educational series for students.

Generally, about one to ten percent of those who pay in advance for an event are no-shows due to personal issues they didn't anticipate. At a paid event, you can usually estimate how many people will attend.

Ask how many tickets they are expecting to sell or how large the space is. From that answer, before accepting the invitation, decide where you will reach more people: from your desk in your office or by speaking publicly.

Also, consider whether the advanced press they are promising is valuable to you. Visibility comes from advance-press; whether people buy tickets or not, they hear about you.

Press Releases

When we started GrantWatch, we couldn't afford to send press releases through a distribution company, so we built our own press email list. We were not successful.

It really is a science how press release companies distribute your release and get it published on thousands of websites. The press release will appear as sponsored, but it does bring in a lot of traffic on that day and new subscribers.

Sending out a press release is not something you should do daily; maybe once a month. We created a barter agreement with a press release company, and we post their press releases in return, related to the grant world on *GrantNews* – a win-win for all.

The Power of Television

As far as getting real news coverage and TV spots, nothing will happen unless you have an advocate who will pitch you and secure 3 to 5 minutes for you.

That is where Hey Sandy and her team came in. Each local TV station has to fill time with human interest, and that could be you – and your name or product can reach thousands instantly.

Even for appearances on podcasts, you need someone to secure those spots, who does that full-time and nothing else. But again, do not waste your time if too few people tune in, or if they have little to no social media presence.

Sometimes, it can be helpful even if they have a small following, if they are willing to give you the edited video to post on your own website and social accounts. But ask that in advance.

I appeared on a news show, or I thought it was, but in the end, it was a gimmick that cost me dearly. The first time, makeup, background, and a new outfit, and I waited 2 hours, and it was cancelled – someone double booked. The second time they filmed it was a great interview, and guess what: to get the film, they had a tiered pricing system. This was the first time I encountered it; only then did I realize it was their business model, and I fell into it. The PR team did not know this either. Live and learn.

That company keeps inviting me back, and I reply that I am happy to fill in your time slot if you send me the video. Otherwise, I am not interested.

Even if you hire someone, do not be a cardboard cutout that is pushed around – ask before you agree. Your time is valuable whether you are an author, artist, entrepreneur, or nonprofit executive.

Face-to-Face Connections

Wherever you go, unless it is a bad hair day or you are just chilling in your running sweats, carry your business cards. You never know who you meet, and every connection is valuable. For me, I can meet a tradesperson at a wedding and then find out that their sister runs a nonprofit – sure, she can call me and pick my brain – here is my card.

Don't be a snob. There are people who call the office and say they once spoke to me 10 years ago, and now they want to reach out and have some questions, and yes, they really do.

I do not necessarily remember them, but after a few minutes on the call, I realized my advice was meaningful and changed the trajectory of their business and career. These are meaningful connections that bring visibility. I wonder how many people the caller had told the story of our conversation to over the past 10 years as he scaled the ladder of success.

Writing Books That Matter

I believe I accomplished this with *The Queen of Grants: From Teacher to Grant Writer to CEO*. From February 1, 2024, through February 17, 2026, 1,006 copies of the first book in the series were purchased on Amazon KDP, along with 23 copies through IngramSpark, and numerous ePub rentals.

It is great to make a difference in so many people's lives. I have friends who self-published and sold only 60 books over 5 years. I know my book makes a difference because I tell my story and teach people at the same time – I am not extraordinary, I am just a regular person who committed to something and followed through. If I can do it, so can you.

Share your journey, and it will give your life meaning and motivate others. It will also help people feel connected to you and your brand.

Website Analytics

Another crucial part of marketing for any nonprofit or business is understanding your analytics. Tracking is vital to growth. Knowing where your website traffic comes from and what people do once they land on your site gives you meaningful insight into where you are succeeding and where you need improvement.

Over the past few years, Google moved from Universal Analytics to GA4. It has more features but is also much more complicated to figure out.

I knew the old Google Analytics inside and out. Now, when I try to use GA4 on my own, I still get lost. And I know I am not the only one. The switch left many businesses stuck, unsure how to interpret their new analytics or what to do with their old data.

At GrantWatch, I waited until Google basically forced the change. Thankfully, I have staff who understand it and keep up with updates as things evolve. They show me where to find the data and which pages to use, and I have some of those pages bookmarked. I know enough to recognize when something is off, such as a drop in unique users, lower engagement, or a higher bounce rate. These are key numbers to check daily.

My marketing team now handles deeper analysis and has taken over most of that work. I am probably being lazy about relearning analytics and will add it to my future goals.

We also use other analytics tools alongside GA4, including Meta analytics for Facebook and Instagram, SEMrush, Google Search Console for SEO, and Google Trends. Together, these help us stay on top of what is happening and better understand what our audience is looking for regarding grants.

I strongly suggest that anyone handling their own in-house marketing ensure they have staff who truly understand analytics, so money is not wasted. Marketing takes up a huge portion of a business's budget, and with the "throw it at the wall and see what sticks" approach, you need someone who can clearly tell you what actually sticks.

The Importance of Good SEO

The importance of good SEO, or search engine optimization, cannot be overstated. You can have great content and provide real value, but if no one can find it, your work won't reach the people who need it. Content only matters when it is discoverable.

Every page on GrantWatch has always been optimized for a specific, high-value keyword so our grants and articles can be found by the right audience. Over the past 25 years, I have handled the SEO myself for most of that time, probably about 75 percent. I hired agencies, worked with different teams, and even had staff members managing it at times, but I kept coming back to it because I wanted it done right. I researched the keywords, placed them where needed, and ensured they appeared not only in the content but also in the page titles and descriptions.

Internal links have also been a big part of our strategy. Linking to our main pages helps visitors navigate the site. It also helps search engines understand where the most important information lives on the website.

Backlinks are just as important. When our press releases and content are shared and linked to by other sites, it builds credibility, not just visibility. Google evaluates websites using its EEAT framework: Experience, Expertise, Authoritativeness, and Trustworthiness. A strong backlink profile and links from reputable sources can signal that a site is trustworthy, which in turn significantly affects rankings.

Today, I am grateful to hand over the SEO responsibilities to Nikita and Ariel. They know what they are doing, and I am hopeful they will stay focused on what truly matters: helping as many people as possible find funding by using GrantWatch.

Running Ads for ROI, Not Just Visibility

Here is a secret that you may not know. Google has agents and advisors who will actually stay on a live call with you and help you publish an ad. Most of them are great. And I am sorry to say I have been ghosting mine lately, and I thank her for her patience while I edit this book. Multitasking does not work while editing.

In my early years in business, I hired different Ad people for Google Ads and Facebook Ads who took a retainer and a percentage of the ad spend. When I hired in-house staff to run the ads, we did much better over the years. But people come and go in the marketing industry, and I was back on my own.

As recently as 2025, I tried again and hired another Ad company that came highly recommended, and the ads did nothing during the 3-month initial contract term. I didn't make any money, and the ads had too much text on the images, so most were disallowed. I am looking for revenue from ads; there needs to be a return on my investment, ROI. It is nice to know about signups and traffic, which the Ad company sent me charts and graphs of, but if it is not converting to ROI, I am not interested.

You would think LinkedIn ads would give a return on investment, but to date, for my industry, they have not. Every year we try again. Instagram ads have visibility but no trackable ROI. We are currently experimenting with X ads and considering TikTok.

Over time, Google has always been the best for us. When I became determined, and I couldn't find a new staff member who I felt knew more than me, I finally rolled up my sleeves and stopped wasting money. I called Google, and I was quick to answer their calls when they wanted to follow up.

Eventually, I learned that before you call Google, get all your assets ready. That would be 20 images, 5 videos. You can have 2 videos in different dimensions, and of the 20 images, you could also have about 7 in each of 3 dimensions. There is no point in listing the sizes here, as they may change; they are available on their website.

You need your words and phrasing, and you can prepare them yourself. It is probably much easier now with AI's help. Each headline and description has a word count and a number indicating how many to prepare. Words are very important on Google because, while we prepare images and videos, your words are often the only things that appear in search results.

You do not need that much money to run ads. I begin an ad with a very small amount. I warm up the ad at $5, and my sweet spot is $10 per ad per day. However, before you start, you need to know upfront what you are tracking. Do you want them to call a number, fill out a form, sign up, or make a payment? What are the possible price points?

Your Google dashboard will tell you something different from what I'm saying. They will tell you to add more funds on your busiest day. I am not a gambler, so my ad spend is conservative and consistent. When you get desperate, just like gamblers, you blow a lot of money, and the more you touch your ads, the less they work.

You need to know who your target audience is. In my next chapter, you will hear how Aaron, our consultant, had my staff define our average customer just so they could understand who they were talking to and address those needs in our content and ads. I plan to revisit that with my team next month. All good ideas should be repeated.

Let's say I have an ad that is producing. I would add an extra dollar to it and wait a while before adding another dollar. It is much better to have 4 ads at $10 each, addressing different needs and clientele, than one ad at $40 a day; this is what I learned the hard way. There have been times when I would purposely upset the algorithm and lower an ad back down to $5 or $10 a day and add the extra to an ad that was producing.

I do not believe in outsourcing advertising or blog articles to marketing companies. I have been there, done that. The original blog posts we received from the outsourcing company way back in 2012 were all fluff – the marketing company did not know our subject matter. My staff is well-trained, communicates via phone and email, and understands consumers' needs. They feel their pain daily, so they are best suited to participate in our marketing.

We have team meetings, and our customer support team speaks with the graphic artists and the blog writers. Until very recently, every employee in the company had to submit at least one blog article a week.

We used to all review the images and posts, but artwork is subjective, so mostly now my team leader approves, and occasionally, once it is live and running, I make it come down for a tweak, the gut instinct again, like too many verbs in a word phrase.

There have been times when, on a Friday of all days, a supervisor was out, and an OMG moment happened when a graphic artist used AI (he has been told not to), and the person had crossed eyes or was missing a finger.

Well, things happen, but less and less often, because the pain of taking something down is worse than the pain of doing it right in the first place.

I want to include a sound bite about Facebook. We are now finally seeing an ROI from Facebook. Do not let anyone tell you Facebook ads are only good for quick traffic. We used to think the same thing until we made it a priority during the 20-Day Platform Challenge and most recently when we hired our Team Lead to further define our customer base.

It took us a long time, but we finally have a Facebook ROI. You need to try many different approaches until you figure out what works for your company.

Targeting the right audience makes all the difference. When we clearly defined our ideal audience using real stories and needs, we heard from our support team, and the many conversations and interviews, combined with data from our customer base, Facebook gave us results that were night and day.

We saw the difference. We are up to a 3X ROI and no longer wasting money. We're no longer throwing money at Facebook ads that don't connect. The difference came from knowing our customers deeply, not from some magic formula.

I read this quote in a novel recently, and I saved it here for this section.

"A good leader lets their staff do what they do best."

Note to self: Stop micromanaging everyone. This is so hard for me because I built this baby, and I want to see it continue well into the future. But even though I am forever young on the book's back cover, I am not, and my staff needs to keep learning and growing.

Creating Your Own Podcast

Besides email and my book, podcasting is my favorite for visibility right now. You need a solid structure for your podcast, something repeatable, with the same theme and framework every time, so you can keep it going without reinventing the wheel each week.

Your podcast must have a clear purpose from the start. I am not going to promise you will monetize it in the first year, because most likely you won't. We still haven't hit the YouTube monetization threshold yet, and unless you are diving into politics, it takes time to build. Many more people watch without subscribing, so growing that subscriber base is a slow-and-steady process.

For me, the purpose was simple: to help grant seekers learn directly from grant funders and recipients, and to share trustworthy B2B pros I have used myself. We get so many questions at GrantWatch, and while we can't have every answer, the collective wisdom from funders and awardees covers a lot.

As of today, in February 2026, we filmed 59 GrantTalk interviews: grant success stories, funding sources, and B2B companies that help nonprofits and businesses grow.

We have edited and published 52 weekly episodes and around 200 shorts. We are also posting our reels on Instagram and TikTok, hoping to reach younger entrepreneurs and executive directors.

Our latest episode, *GrantTalk* Episode 52 with Soon Hagerty, Co-founder and President of Boundless Futures Foundation, on fueling women founders with grit, grants, and guidance, is already getting solid views and sparking great conversations in the comments from folks looking for that kind of inspiration.

This ties right back to the bigger picture: when people know your name in a positive way through consistent, valuable content like *GrantTalk*, growth happens naturally. It builds trust and attracts business.

At GrantWatch, it helped strengthen our subscription model and sustain our mission. Podcasting is one part of showing up every day in people's feeds, but when combined with the rest of your efforts, it helps your name stick.

At the end of the day, people need to know your name. If they don't know your name, they can't find you. And if they can't find you, nothing else matters. Visibility is the whole game.

III: The 20-Day Platform Challenge

The reason this chapter of our history made it into this book is to illustrate what it actually took to turn a fully functioning website and business established in 2010 into what it is today and what it is becoming.

In Chapter One, you heard from funders, grant awardees, and B2B partners. Here, you will hear the voices of GrantWatch staff who, through their daily journaling, share the work behind the updates to our website platform and marketing, and how the process helped us build a stronger culture, one where ideas are welcomed, and team members take ownership of their tasks and results.

What Prompted the Challenge?

I tell my grandchildren that "Change is a process, not an event." I confess that I was not always as open to change as I was in April 2025. Why? Because I was so deep in the muck of day-to-day operations, putting out fires, I was not looking objectively at my business from the outside. Every customer issue, social post, blog article review, or slow server speed took over my day.

I ate at my desk and had 15-hour workdays. If my husband didn't bring me food, I would have lived on chocolate and coffee.

They say that a business leader must make time every day to work "on" their business, rather than "in" it. I, however, didn't see the need for change or have time for it, and I was just too busy, and I stayed stuck.

When anyone suggested a change, I felt, "What do they know? I already live, breathe, and sleep my business. How much more can I do?"

And that was another issue. I had made organizational charts, but everyone's job overlapped too much to follow.

The April 2025 holidays came too quickly, (the story of my life – they always seem to creep up out of nowhere) and after working as hard as I had been, publishing by then 4 original children's books and 3 accompanying activity and coloring books from December 2024 to March 2025, I put my proverbial foot down and announced to my family, "I am not cooking, entertaining, having company, or staying home for the holidays." I finally found a program, and we did get the last rooms available.

By the time we booked the holiday conference program for myself and some family, I had already written about half of this book, *The*

Queen of Grants 2, completed the text of a fifth children's book, and sent it off for illustration. I sincerely needed to power down.

And yet, I signed up to be a speaker at the conference and share my experience as a new indie children's book author. I even brought along coloring pages that accompany the storybooks, for the children attending the day camp at the conference.

Besides speaking, I attended other sessions and met three prominent people, each with a much larger social following than we did. My mailing list was what amazed them, whereas my social media (even though we posted valuable content daily) was a pittance in comparison.

I couldn't understand why, with 43 podcasts by that date, we hadn't even reached 3k watch hours on YouTube and were sitting at only 3,000 followers.

While this was puzzling me, I met a young man named Aaron on a boat ride who was filming the event and would later post a composite video on the program's social media accounts. My daughter, Lianne, pushed me daily to fully introduce myself and to ask for a meeting.

We ended up having several meetings in which Aaron shared his impressions of my website. He told me that it looked like we had developed it many years ago and that it needed "a full refresh."

OMG is all my brain could say. I cannot begin to tell you how that made me feel. However painful, I took it all under advisement.

We talked about his branding ideas, and my head was spinning. So much for relaxation – but I appreciated his candor. I do not impress easily, but I was feeling like WOW! I think I found my semi-retirement strategy – some call it an exit strategy.

However, Aaron was not looking for a full-time position because his marketing agency was quickly stacking clients.

I, on the other hand, want my staff to be fully engaged and dedicated to the project. I felt confident that he would make a difference. My husband, who has been down this road before, where we get promises and no delivery because the consultant has many clients, was reserving judgment.

I had room in my budget because, until Queen 2 was finished, I was not resigning with Hey Sandy, our PR company.

The pundits say that developing a habit takes 21 consecutive days, and with weekends and holidays, a Monday-to-Friday office doesn't have 21 consecutive workdays to do so.

But what we did have time to develop was a clearer vision, a more positive attitude, and a company culture that included staff ideas and values. Everyone's ideas would matter, and staff would be heard.

Aaron and I agreed to a one-month remote consultancy: 5 mornings a week for 20 workdays, 60 hours, and one flight to Florida for a filming day to train our videographer.

I wanted my staff to develop sales and marketing habits. I wanted it to become a mindset and integral to their work at GrantWatch. I also wanted them to review the website pages objectively while involved, speak up, and identify where consumers might have issues.

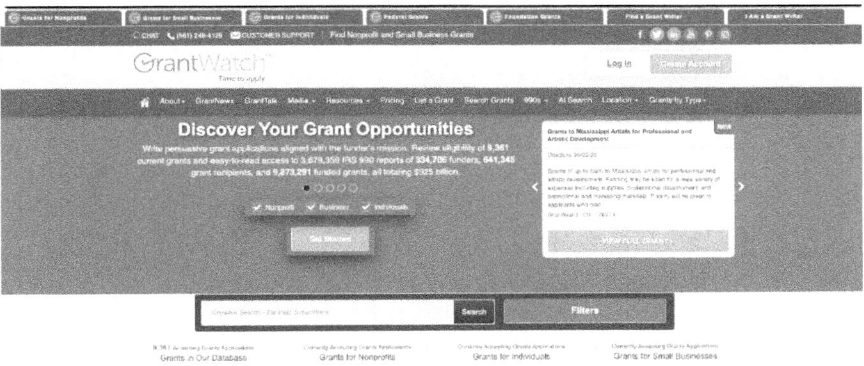

We got home on Tuesday, April 22nd, and Aaron began working the following week. No part of the business would be spared from Aaron's involvement and creativity. This is where we began the 20-

Day Platform Challenge: Monday, April 28th, on Aaron's first workday.

To avoid negative anticipation, I hinted on Friday afternoon that there would be a few changes on Monday. Nothing was said about the whirlwind of activity we were about to endure.

Thus, we had Aaron for twenty days of change. And to say change is an understatement.

I started writing this chapter on the eve of Day 8, and by then, we had a revised content calendar, a new Instagram strategy, and the home page, search page, and the "All Grants" page had already had their Bootstrap upgraded, and our home page had the beginning of a totally new vibe.

We were working on an SEO chart, upgrading the category pages, and we rewrote all the content for the new home page. Oh yes, we kept our logo but reinvigorated the colors.

We were introduced to Bolt.new, which was very helpful for coding the new web pages with appropriate prompts. We'd also been introduced to Capcut, which would take our long videos and cut them into reels of great content.

And I must say again: "change is a process, not an event," but ours was turbo-charged, and most of the staff involved in the challenge were working with Aaron, giving us A+ 200% creativity and follow-through. And I believe my team deserves a very loud shout-out!

I decided to let them tell their story through a 20-Day Platform Challenge journal. I wanted you to understand what a challenge like this could mean for your employees and your company.

We are rethinking what our customers need, how they interact with us, what brings them in and turns them out, and how we engage with them on social media.

My staff became so invested that when I ask the developer to make a change to a page that they worked on the day before, they want to know what happened. Why did I change it? And it feels like a personal win when the idea they have suggested many times gets put up there.

Meetings can be chaotic because we are working on several projects with specialized staff members, and each one needs a few minutes. I had to tell a staff member that I can let them talk more at meetings after the 20 days because I needed to hear Aaron's opinion. That felt bad, and as I lay my head on my pillow that night, I realized I may have pushed her aside, but as I said, meetings do get chaotic. I am going to drop her a Teams "So sorry message."

Remember, we still had to run the company, handle customer service, send out grant alerts and blog articles, work with our grant associate office to post the grants, publish articles, and post to social media; so there was no break in service. We also had to test any new changes before they went live, so our customers could continue using the live website.

To give you some context on when this happened, Skype, which my company has used since its inception for in-house communication, was going down, and Teams, which I was using as a guest user, was taking over. We can no longer record, as we were using Google Workspace accounts. And while we knew in advance, I was publishing books before the holiday and came home to prep for Aaron's arrival at our company.

We held most meetings on Zoom, with people coming and going as needed, and then moved to Teams after Aaron left at noon. All day, we were busy with our tasks, and I found myself jumping in and out of meetings, with my approval requested at every turn. The staff was working really hard, and I am so proud of them.

Here goes. The good, the bad, and the pain process are all exposed for you to learn from our experience. Everyone reacts to change differently, and also to having to cover for someone else, while they are more heavily involved in the change process.

Day 1: Monday

♟ Sue, Executive Office Manager

Aaron's Introduction: Monday began on a high note with Aaron's arrival, who brought not only a personable and engaging demeanor but also a wealth of talent and insight. He is here to help elevate our social media presence and enhance our website, key steps toward expanding the business we're all so passionate about.

It was both a pleasure and a surprise to meet someone so young with such exceptional qualities and skills. Aaron's presence is truly a gift, and it was incredibly refreshing to witness his professionalism and drive. Kudos to his parents for instilling such admirable values and clearly passing along great genes.

What stood out most was his no-nonsense approach; he jumped right into business from the start, and we're grateful for that kind of initiative.

◎ Aaron, Strategic Consultant

Customer Portfolio Analysis: I held initial meetings with the incredible team at GrantWatch, completed onboarding, and introduced and integrated social media software to optimize our data collection and social media posting. The team began discussing the company's ideal client, persona, and target audience to curate an effective marketing strategy and avatar. Nikita's apparent grasp of this process greatly assisted with implementation, and Lori was incredibly quick to understand the newly implemented software.

📊 Nikita, Data Analyst / Media Manager

Mondays are my favorite day at GrantWatch. They're busy and fast-paced, the perfect time for my superstar skills to shine. Since it's typically the most hectic day of the week, I take pride in being efficient and accurate, stepping up to help lighten the load for the rest of the team.

Today, I tackled the bulk of the support inbox, allowing Danika to focus on failed payments, Pamela to manage multi-user accounts, and Sue to focus on refund requests and Stripe disputes. Most of the emails I handled involved assisting customers with various queries, calming frustrations when people couldn't find the right grants, and redirecting those who aren't a good fit to resources like Benefits.gov.

We also had a team meeting with Aaron to discuss our new social media management tool - Metricool.com. It looks promising, but it's not without flaws. Some posts still require manual work directly on the social platforms. I plan to explore it further tomorrow and am genuinely curious to see whether it can help us streamline our social media efforts.

💻 Chris, Web Developer

Starting Fresh: Today, I started working on the new frontend for GrantWatch. Nikita gave me a clear list of tasks, which helped me know where to begin. I focused on creating a clean layout that is easier to manage and modify later. The old design was hard to work with because everything was too mixed together. I had a call with Aaron, and he gave me some good advice on keeping things simple and clean. I worked a bit late because I was excited to get started.

💡 Pamela, Customer Support Specialist

We have a new consultant. I wonder what to expect. Excited to see that we will be making changes. Our consultant, Aaron, seems very knowledgeable and works quickly. I wonder if he will be on the same page as we are.

🌀 Danika, Grant Support Specialist

Introductions: We met as individuals but immediately became collaborators. The first conversations with Aaron set the tone: excitement, respect, and a clear understanding that we were about to do important work, work that would reflect the heart and future of our brand.

✍ Lori, Editor and Media Manager

Monday was a whirlwind. I found out about the new software, Metricool, minutes before the meeting, which left me feeling a little disoriented. Still, I adapted quickly. Aaron's energy during the initial walkthrough was both motivational and overwhelming at times. He's clearly passionate, but I felt a slower-paced, instructional tone might have made the introduction more digestible.

I contributed by actively listening, absorbing what I could, and reviewing the site on my own time to prepare for the week ahead. I downloaded and explored the site that evening to begin learning the layout.

🎨 Adrian, Graphic Artist

I haven't made personal logs in a long while. I had the impression that I was making work logs at first. Turns out it'll have a little more personality than that.

Let's get started then. Image posting is as usual: I create the content and send it for approval, or they make changes. The foundational postings for the future images are being set up, leaving a canvas for applying the suggestions. We're going to have someone come in to help with the entire GrantWatch ecosystem. He'll meet with everyone and get an idea of what we do.

📹 Andre, Videographer

The first day began with no motion, but with waiting. My computer, my tool, my tether to creation– gone. My hard drive crashed over the weekend, and I brought it in for repair.

I imagined all that could be done… If only I had access to my computer.

But I could only wait, and in the wait, I wondered: Was this a part of a cosmic lesson? Sometimes the first step toward a new beginning is stillness.

✉ David, Email Marketing Consultant

The day started with a request from Libby to do some Microsoft Excel data cleaning, which I eagerly did as it was a different task from my regular programmed schedule, a change in my routine, which is always a good thing. Also, we had our first request to fill and update a spreadsheet of our daily tasks. I figured it was to be a timetable designed for teamwork with our new consultant. It was a wild guess, but just at that moment, it felt right.

🗨 Jeff, Writer - In the Beginning

There Was the End: For me, the beginning of my story today is actually the end...at least for the current article I'm working on. I still need to polish my article so it's as good as possible. I'm not sure who is actually reading them (my articles) once they're published, but I write each article as a 'story' that I enjoy and am satisfied with.

It's also interesting that someone has been brought on for a short-term, intensive effort to improve the company's operations. I'll have to see how that unfolds.

Day 2: Tuesday

♟ Sue, Executive Office Manager

Chaos Day: Despite a day full of added complications, such as Vonage issues and navigating vendor forms, Aaron remained focused and productive, diving right into tasks and implementing meaningful changes. His energy never wavered, and the impact of his work was clear. The staff responded positively to him, with smooth Zoom sessions and wonderful cooperation. There were no complaints or conflicts; instead, every team member felt heard, and their input was genuinely considered.

🎯 Aaron, Strategic Consultant

Graphic Creation Process: The team led by Libby, assisted by Lori, Sue, Nikita, Danika, and Pamela, continued analyzing company data through the newly integrated software while introducing team-wide discussions in which members incorporated their personal experiences with clients to address customer frustrations and appreciation, and to define authentic clientele. Effectively defining an avatar and understanding priorities in optimization to improve customer experience and immediately optimize conversions.

Sue, Pamela, and Danika were especially helpful in site development, drawing on years of personal experience to help our customer support center understand and present the most pressing customer needs and suggest necessary improvements.

We met with the development team and Adrian, our in-house graphic designer, to introduce a new, modern graphics style consistent with the developing social media strategy led by Lori and Nikita, while simultaneously giving a crash course on the importance of consistent branding, strategy, and a customer-centric perspective for effective results.

📊 Nikita, Data Analyst / Media Manager

Today I spent more time exploring Metricool.com and ran a few test posts to get a better feel for the platform. The highlight of my day, though, was our meeting with Aaron to review what makes a social media post most effective. It was incredibly validating to hear him emphasize many of the strategies I've advocated over the years, particularly the importance of using strong hooks and more engaging content.

Our current social media efforts haven't been as impactful as they could be. I've often felt like my enthusiasm for creativity and storytelling isn't always matched by the rest of the team. Whether it's a difference in energy, vision, or just creative bandwidth, it's been frustrating at times. But now that Aaron is echoing these ideas, I'm hopeful it will help shift the mindset and elevate the overall quality of our social media output.

I was also glad to find that Aaron shares my perspective on social media advertising. We both agree that the budget could be better spent elsewhere, specifically on hiring an additional skilled developer. Fixing the ongoing site issues more efficiently would not only improve the user experience but also boost customer retention.

It's a short workday for me today. I have to head to the hospital later for my plasma infusion treatments, an essential but exhausting part of keeping me alive. Here's hoping everything goes smoothly.

📖 Chris, Web Developer

Building the Navigation: I worked on the main menu to make it easier to use. Nikita had already told me it needed to be better. I followed some of Aaron's ideas and created a simple version we can improve later. I also fixed a few layout issues across different screen sizes. Libby set up a meeting with the whole team. Everyone offered helpful ideas for the design, such as improving spacing between elements and using nicer fonts. I feel good about the progress we are making.

💡 Pamela, Customer Support Specialist

I see changes are being made. How exciting. He seems to be taking our thoughts and needs into consideration. I wonder what GrantWatch will look like. I'm glad Libby brought him on board.

◐ Danika, Grant Support Specialist

Anticipation: The conversations were full of ideas, creative thinking, and a genuine commitment to better marketing the brand's true voice. There was a real sense of teamwork in knowing we were building a future we could all stand behind. We came together around a shared mission: to honor the brand while elevating the user experience.

✍ Lori, Editor and Media Manager

Tuesday's session with Nikita was insightful but felt too short. As an educator with a Master's in Rhetoric and Writing, I was hoping for a deeper dive into the platform's practical application, especially its connection to our ad content strategy. We had a valuable conversation about audience and purpose, but we needed more time to apply those concepts in a hands-on way. While we didn't finish a sample post, I took the initiative to complete the assigned "homework" of drafting GWT (Grant Writer Team) ad image copy. That exercise helped me channel what I'd learned into real output and push the campaign in a new, clearer direction.

🎨 Adrian, Graphic Artist

The mapping of the way postings have begun. A good number of ideas were suggested. I'd say the usual routine will change a lot. The social media images will be handled differently to separate the article image from the rest, and I will send the rest for approval. That'll make the process a bit longer, but if it helps, so be it. It was a productive Zoom meeting, I'd say. Seems like a good foundation for what needs to be done.

🎥 Andre, Videographer

I set out to retrieve my computer, the lifeline to my craft. Time pressed against my shoulders like a Florida storm surge; every minute away from the desk was a minute lost to progress.

I arrived at Best Buy of Boynton Beach with an unwavering focus, driven by urgency. I met with the Geek Squad worker at the front desk. She was poised and graceful, smiling at me with kind eyes that lingered. She extended my laptop toward me, our fingers grazed, and when the laptop was in my hands, the weight of it was like a sword to a knight before battle.

I returned with my device just in time to join the Zoom meeting for the new Social Media Manager's arrival. The moment we had all anticipated. We spoke. Briefly but intentionally. He shared tools, ideas, and fragments of a strategy that hinted at structure. Each point landed like a note in a song that was the theme for GrantWatch as a whole.

And then– He said he'd call me tomorrow. At that moment, it felt like the beginning of a partnership with structures and blueprints of an upward trajectory. Tomorrow's promised call will reveal a new direction. Day 3 was coming...And with purpose.

✉ David, Email Marketing Consultant

I still did not fully understand at that moment what was required to fill regarding our Teamwork, as my task as an Email Marketing Consultant are often not related to other staff members work, sometimes I joke with the concept that it is like the Snow White story, I am in the mine far from the castle, doing E-mail Data Mining and Processing Data Diamonds.

🗨 Jeff, Writer

And so, it starts anew: I finished my latest story - er, I mean article, about Housing Grants. Some topics are more important than others, and this is one of those articles. Afterall, the grants listed are there to help find (grant) funding to start - or possibly finish - some kind of housing project. There are usually 10-20 grants per article. This article lists 12 grants. I am always hopeful that at least someone (or some organization) will derive benefit from one of these grants.

It looks like there are a number of things happening on the company efficiency front, but most of it doesn't involve me - at least not directly. A lot of social media stuff is intended to help make it easier for people to access our site and its resources.

Day 3: Wednesday

♟ Sue, Executive Office Manager

Another Chaotic Day: Wednesday brought more trials and tribulations as Nikita wasn't available because her grandmother had taken a spill and was hospitalized. Amidst all of this, we continued working with Pushpendra to resolve the ongoing email and cron issues. The day became increasingly hectic as I had to divide my attention between unresolved staff concerns, customer support, phone calls, chats, and prioritizing urgent matters. My approach in these situations is always to remain calm and focused, addressing the most critical issues first. Despite the challenges, we accomplished a great deal with Aaron and made significant progress in just a few short days.

🎯 Aaron, Strategic Consultant

Website Renovation: The day began with a meeting with Andre, the video editor, to discuss implementing AI software to significantly improve content-creation efficiency.

Later, in a team-wide meeting with the development team, we addressed immediate necessary improvements to the website and social media. I incorporated marketing strategy and AI software to create models for an improved site while maintaining the brand's identity and site functionality.

📊 Nikita, Data Analyst / Media Manager

Today I'm at home recovering from my plasma infusion treatments, so I wasn't able to go to work. I'm hoping everything is running smoothly in my absence, and I'm looking forward to getting back soon to catch up on the progress the team has made. It's always tough to be away, but I'm grateful for the support and excited to return with fresh energy.

💻 Chris, Web Developer

Homepage Layout: Today, I worked on the homepage structure. I rebuilt the banner area and added sections for featured grants. Nikita sent some notes that helped me know what content needed to be shown first. Aaron gave feedback on colors and spacing. I started using reusable components to save time on future pages. I also tested how it looks on mobile. It's starting to feel more real now.

💡 Pamela, Customer Support Specialist

Changes are coming together. I love seeing that some of my ideas for simplifying our search are being put into practice.

⚙ Danika, Grant Support Specialist

 Finding Our Focus: Some people hadn't yet seen the bigger picture Libby was aiming for. They didn't fully understand how Libby could be an influencer while still aligning with the website's brand. Some of the team were still unsure how we could achieve success by yielding to the user profile Aaron provided. However, for some of us, the goal has always been the same: to form a cohesive experience for our current users while also expanding its reach and inspiring a wider audience.

✍ Lori, Editor and Media Manager

Wednesday took an unexpected turn. While I was hoping to complete our Metricool tutorial and review my ad homework, the schedule changed due to a family emergency. I was instead invited to a website development session. While this isn't my wheelhouse, I actively listened and occasionally asked questions, gaining invaluable insight into the design process. I contributed by maintaining a steady presence and multitasking with other work while the development team flowed seamlessly. Susan, Danika, and Pamela's collaboration was inspiring. It taught me a lot about functional redesign, user experience, and how passionate people build something great together.

🎨 Adrian, Graphic Artist

GrantWriterTeam had some suggestions on how to approach the wording in the future. It was suggested using wording that entices viewers to learn how to become a grant writer, or, alternatively, where to hire one. This was an approach to creating these images, a departure from the way things were before.

There was a point in the meeting that stuck out to me. The postings for *GrantWriterTeam* before Aaron were described as making content for the sake of making content. I can't say I disagreed. I roll with what the business wants and follow the previous designer's lead. I learned in the meeting that there wasn't much engagement with these posts. Basically, changing the entire idea of what the images are. While it's good to make content that'll appeal to the type of person we want engaged, I'll kind of miss the puns.

🎥 Andre, Videographer

We had our first real team meeting. The new hire shared his screen and introduced us to Metricool, a platform that analyzes social media content performance using engagement metrics. The data wasn't just numbers– it told a story.

Then it happened. He said, "We need to define our avatar." And like that, the meeting shifted, and the air changed.

The image emerged of a 38-year-old businesswoman who is focused and composed, stylish and classy.

She wasn't just our target– she was our standard. From this point forward, everything we created had to resonate with her.

The tone, the polish, the rhythm of every video– each decision had to answer one question: Would she care?

She made everything feel real. No longer abstract or experimental. It wasn't just content, it was communication. Every video is a message directly to her.

✉ David, Email Marketing Consultant

Something was going on our Webpage design but I was fully focused on my daily tasks and our chats were not giving me a clue on what was going with the rest of the team, however I was thinking to myself on a previous request from a document done by Libby on which she suggested that if we had no team work, at least we could suggest improvements on our daily tasks and I had so many ideas that I have been considering for so long.

💬 Jeff, Writer

On to the Next One: Now I need to start writing a new article. Fortunately, I usually have a solid title or theme that's listed in our schedule. Sometimes I modify the title if I think of a way to tweak it. It might be because I found a better angle, or maybe I thought of a pithy way to spice up the title so that even more people will read it.

As far as these daily entries, I don't want any of my entries to be more than 200 words - give or take a few - so I can be as concise as possible while still conveying the intended message.

Day 4: Thursday

♟ Sue, Executive Office Manager

A Tremendous Day: Nikita has been a rock star throughout the week, offering valuable insights and creative ideas. She consistently brought thoughtful suggestions to the table, many of which she ran by me before sharing them with Aaron for review. I'm pleased to say that several of her ideas have already been implemented. The rest of the staff also contributed several smart, well-considered suggestions, making it a highly productive day.

◎ Aaron, Strategic Consultant

Team Lead Renovation: Working hand in hand with the developers Chris and Pushpendra, the team led by Libby, assisted by Sue, Nikita, Danika, Pamela, and Lori, continued to improve the website's functionality, modernization, and user experience. Edits were made as the team continued to incorporate data and personal experience into the improved GrantWatch site.

🔳 Nikita, Data Analyst / Media Manager

I'm back at work today, and WOW - huge news: the homepage is getting a makeover! This is such a big moment for me personally because I've been advocating for a redesign since I first joined the company. For years, I kept an Excel sheet tracking customer emails and chats, carefully logging each topic and analyzing the data. The results were consistent: customers found the homepage overwhelming and didn't know where to start. A more user-friendly experience has been long overdue, and I'm thrilled that change is finally happening. I'm eager to share my insights and data to help shape a homepage that truly serves our users' needs.

One of my tasks today was to gather the best customer success stories to feature on the new homepage. It was a nostalgic process revisiting them - so many meaningful stories! It was hard to choose, but I ultimately selected ones that highlight different strengths of the platform: first-time grant recipients, the affordable value of GrantWatch.com, the depth of information in our grant detail pages, and the overall importance of using a dedicated grant search directory like ours.

This is a step in the right direction, and I can't wait to see how the new homepage evolves.

📓 Chris, Web Developer: Search and Filters:

I spent most of the day working on the search bar and filter section. These are important for users seeking specific grants. I used Aaron's ideas to make the filter look clean and easy to use. Nikita checked everything and said it looked much better than before. I still need to connect it to the real data later, but the structure is ready.

💡 Pamela, Customer Support Specialist

Some changes to the homepage. Uh oh... It's a little too bright. But I have hopes it will come together.

🌀 Danika, Grant Support Specialist

Collaboration: Everything changed when we built together in real time. Working side by side, we designed, adapted, and innovated in real time. We listened. We trusted our colleagues and created with purpose and precision. Suddenly, the project no longer felt theoretical. It felt tangible and exciting. The new designs were not just better; they were true to the brand's identity. Together, we built a user experience that was welcoming to our current and potential users.

 Lori, Editor and Media Manager

Thursday was productive and energizing. I joined Nikita and Danika to write SEO-rich scripts for upcoming social media reels; short, punchy, engaging content based on our highest-performing articles. It was great to brainstorm with a team that understands both content and marketing. We drafted scripts and contributed ideas, then I shifted back to my daily tasks while Nikita polished our final output. This was a strong example of focused collaboration and team synergy.

Adrian, Graphic Artist

I want to modify the images I created to comply with the changes suggested in the meetings. There were a lot of images to get through to change. This task will have to continue to the next day with the required amount. It must be emphasized that I'll need to go through so many images. This will be a lengthy process, but it is necessary. I usually like to be ahead of the requested images so I don't have to work at the last minute. Especially since the new work will take priority over the previous. Having everything not piled up on one day is something I like to avoid. Having to go back and change everything kind of upends that. I hope it doesn't catch up to me, but I'll do what I can.

🎥 Andre, Videographer

These were more routine editing days for *GrantTalk* episodes and reels, but I also noticed the team using a shared content calendar and pre-written scripts. That system is incredibly useful for keeping things efficient and well-organized.

✉ David, Email Marketing Consultant

Even as I still had not done anything different from my daily chores, I was very worried about what would happen next Monday, 5/5, when Skype phased out.

💬 Jeff, Writer - On to the Next One

You see this title? Some people might recognize this as being a slight variation of a Dolly Parton song. I'm thinking maybe one or two people might (at least) get a chuckle out of that. Once I have the article in mind, I go ahead and plug it into the program we use to write and publish our articles. The title is not always completely original, but I usually change at least a few words so it stands out on its own!

Day 5: Friday

♟ Sue, Executive Office Manager

Leaps and Bounds: Today marked another major step forward, both in progress and in mindset. One of the most appreciated aspects of this experience has been the openness with which suggestions have been received and, more importantly, the number that have already been implemented. It's incredibly motivating for the team to feel that their input matters.

There had been a misconception among some that Libby might be hesitant about modernizing the website. But I always knew that wasn't the case; she simply believes in a thoughtful, phased approach. Change doesn't have to be overwhelming; it can happen steadily, with purpose. And now, as we add the necessary updates to stay current and competitive, it's clear that this transformation is being approached with both care and enthusiasm.

Despite a few unrelated technical hiccups throughout the week, the strides we made in modernizing and streamlining the website were significant. It's rewarding to see tangible results from everyone's hard work and collaboration as we continue moving the platform forward.

🎯 Aaron, Strategic Consultant

Content Creation Process: On Friday, we continued site optimization as the easy-to-use and modern website came together. After the final touches, I led the social media team through a professional content-creation process that used AI, their creativity, and an avatar. While implementing the developed social media strategy, they learned a new system for developing scripts and content.

Lori and Nikita did an excellent job in this process, displaying their obvious grasp of social media and creativity.

📊 Nikita, Data Analyst / Media Manager

Today's meeting with Aaron was focused on developing customer avatars for GrantWatch. It was a valuable discussion, and while I won't be the primary user, I really hope Andre and Lori take this seriously and incorporate the insights into their work moving forward.

My main task today was writing social media scripts, with a focus on reels since they tend to be the most engaging. I put a lot of thought and effort into them, but their success will really depend on strong execution. A great videographer and a compelling influencer are key here, so I'm hopeful that Adrian and Libby will collaborate well to bring the vision to life.

On the homepage redesign front, things felt a bit chaotic - too many cooks in the kitchen today. With so many people offering input, we lost momentum trying to perfect minor details like wording. While progress was made, I couldn't help but feel that too much time was spent on tweaks that will likely change again later. I wish there were more focus on the core functionality, which is the most time-sensitive and impactful part of the project.

Chris, Web Developer

Listing Page Update: I focused on the grants listing page today. I updated the card design and added better spacing. I also worked on hover effects and tested different fonts. Nikita reminded me to keep things simple and clear for users. I started preparing for pagination, but I haven't finished it yet. It was a long day, but I liked how the page was starting to look.

Pamela, Customer Support Specialist

The new blue looks much better on the home page. Glad to see we now have a direction for our branding and social media. I like the way our Instagram posts look now.

Danika, Grant Support Specialist

Momentum: We agreed that as a team, we could amplify the brand's voice in new and authentic ways. With the website design heading in the right direction, the marketing strategy could now be transformed.

Lori, Editor and Media Manager

On Friday, I was tasked with recovering a missing URL from *GrantNews*. I used every search term and method I could think of, but was unsuccessful. It was frustrating, but I stayed committed to the task. Later, I helped test the site redesign. The new layout felt clean, modern, and far more user-friendly. While I wasn't a fan of some of the new color choices, I understood that user testing would ultimately determine what works. My feedback focused on usability and accessibility. Despite visual preferences, I'm very excited to work with this new, improved platform.

Adrian, Graphic Artist

Continuing from the previous day, I needed to modify the remaining images and perform the regular duties. The foundations from before were set, and I had a canvas to change the wording and composition. It was also on this day that I continued making new images, visiting stock sites, and selecting a group of images to use and edit. I must mention that finding images that fit the mood or point of what it's attached to is pretty time-consuming. If the images don't pass muster, I'll go back and look for something new, with added direction on what the image should be. There are many images from when I was first brought on. I was tasked with finding suitable images for a bunch of articles. It's a familiar process at this point, let's just say. Sometimes, when the image has a very specific direction, rather than spending a lot of time looking and finding nothing, I just combine images to fit a composition. I have fun making things like that, but it is no short process, and they usually want quick turnarounds. So, I do this process very sparingly. Oh well.

🎥 Andre, Videographer

I was introduced to Opusclip, and it changed everything. It has streamlined the editing process for reels and shorts: less time scrubbing through footage, more time creating and generating interesting b-roll. It helps add a sharp visual style, especially with captions. It's been a tool I'm glad to have, as it's leveled up my efficiency and creativity.

✉ David, Email Marketing Consultant

Still worried about the upcoming changes on Skype, I have reached out to Susan a few times, and I look forward to being prepared for the dreaded day when we have to change how our team communicates.

🧠 Jeff, Writer

 What Grants to Include? It may sound like an easy question, but the answer is a little more involved. With a directory of over 9,000 grant listings, it may seem like a daunting task!

Fortunately, there are many ways to narrow the search. Grants are divided into 60 different categories, from Aging and Seniors to Youth and At-Risk Youth. A great improvement on our new home page is that each grant category now includes a brief overview of the types of grants in that category. But the best part (at least for me) is that each category also lists HOW MANY grants are listed in that category. It's nice to know upfront the size of the potential grant pool in each category. Since I comb through most, if not all, of the grants in preparation to write my articles, it's helpful to have a good idea of the scope of the grant category being researched.

Day: 5.5 Sunday

📊 Nikita, Data Analyst / Media Manager

I don't usually work on Sundays, but tomorrow is a big day for Libby, and the website renovation still needs significant improvements to deliver the user experience we're aiming for. So today, I teamed up with Chris to make some key updates. I started by sending him a list of necessary changes to the site's footer. We managed to knock those out before he had to head out. I'll pick things up again tomorrow, but I'm genuinely excited - we're making real progress.

Day 6: Monday

🏆 Sue, Executive Office Manager

Preparing for Filming: Today was an interesting day! Aaron was on Zoom with our staff at the airport before he flew to Florida to join the podcast experience and offer input. He and Andre set everything up in Florida for Tuesday's filming.

I also sent the research to Libby for the 3 *GrantTalk* podcasts so she can prepare for interviewing the guests.

Though we experienced a slight delay in the morning while developers resolved a customer login issue, the team made solid progress in key areas. One of our major accomplishments was the successful implementation of the Featured Grants section, which now offers a cleaner, more engaging presentation to users. We also finalized the enhanced search functionality at the top of the homepage, making it faster and more intuitive for visitors to find relevant grant listings.

🎯 Aaron, Strategic Consultant – Sunny Skies:

Monday began from an Airline Lounge as I made my way to Palm Beach to meet the team and assist in the filming process. As I landed in Palm Beach, Andre, the film director, and I worked together to create a new filming setting with improved lighting and professionalism for short-form, long-form, and podcast filming. The new setting is unlike the previous one and presents a much more professional image and a better representation of GrantWatch.

Nikita and Chris continued working into the night to improve the site and produce a final product; both demonstrated a strong work ethic and positive energy, enabling quick, efficient, and professional development. When necessary, I stepped in to offer input or give assistance.

📊 Nikita, Data Analyst / Media Manager

Mondays are always the busiest at GrantWatch. And today was no exception. With a flood of support tickets in our inbox and Libby filming her big project, the pressure was on to keep the momentum going with the website renovations. I'm working closely with Chris again, and we set some ambitious goals for the day.

Our priorities included fixing the website menu, correcting color inconsistencies, adding a link to the 990s on the homepage, highlighting top success stories, optimizing their images, and creating fresh meta tags for over 60 grant categories. On top of that, we're still dealing with a major issue: the homepage search function is down, and it's critical that we resolve it as soon as possible.

It felt like we were putting out fires all day. In addition to website tasks, I handled password resets, assisted the support team with the inbox, and used SEMrush to research SEO strategies and refine keyword-rich meta descriptions for each grant category.

Just when I thought the day couldn't get any busier, Libby threw in a curveball, two brand new pages: one for funding sources and another for recipient types. Those will have to wait until tomorrow.

It was a long, intense day, but the progress Chris and I made feels substantial. I'm exhausted but energized, ready to hit the ground running again tomorrow.

Chris, Web Developer

Starting the Grant Search Page: I began working on the grant search page today. This is the page users go to after adding filters on the homepage. I updated the whole page from Bootstrap 3 to Bootstrap 5. I also changed the header and cleaned up the page layout. The new design looks much cleaner and more modern now. I will continue doing the same for the rest of the pages.

Pamela, Customer Support Specialist

Seeing improvements. The new look of our site is coming together. We still need to tweak our new search function. As a customer support specialist, my purpose is to make it easy for the subscriber to find grants that meet their goals.

Danika, Grant Support Specialist

Commitment to Success: Weekend disruptions shook the team's morale. Suddenly, the site went live before the team's quality checks were completed. It was frustrating because we all cared so much about getting it right. However, even in that moment, the bigger truth was undeniable: Fixes will happen, improvements will roll out, because we are all invested in success.

Because of the spirit, resilience, and shared ownership that this team has shown. We built the next chapter of our brand's story, and we are excited about GrantWatch's future growth.

🖋️ Lori, Editor and Media Manager

I sat in on the developer call. While I mainly listened and observed, I also provided some input on the site as I continued with my regular work throughout the meeting.

🎨 Adrian, Graphic Artist

It was suggested that the words in the social media images have more space between them. Article images can remain brief and punchy, while social media posts can be catchier and more informative to capture viewers' attention, necessitating a reevaluation of how they are worded. So instead of short captions, they need to be informative and entice viewers to click the images. I'll need to punch up the wording and get those eyes on what we post. Sure, let's do this. I mean, I'll need to go back and change those images again, but that's what is needed to help GrantWatch. I also made a GIF for the website. I chose a better image and made a flashy little GIF. Very reminiscent of how websites used them back in the early days of images. This needed a fast turnaround, so I updated the elements and sent them to the website editors. Gifs. Many people online can make animated GIFs, and so do I. I use it to show off my animated works. I haven't made a GIF in a while, but I still remember how to. Change of pace, I suppose.

🎥 Andre, Videographer

I met the new hire in person and got hands-on experience with a new camera setup technique that adds depth to visual content– an insightful addition to the workflow. It gave me a better understanding of how to elevate the visual quality of our content.

✉ David, Email Marketing Consultant

During our first Zoom call about website changes, all team members were required to test, and I checked several variables. The website looked so modern and different; I was excited about the direction it was taking with its visuals. I had waited so long for those changes.

🧠 Jeff, Writer - Preschool Article Almost Complete

It took some time today, but I'm getting there. Today, I put the finishing touches on my current article about Preschool grants. Two things to do before my final review. The first is to insert a proper

Meta Description. This is a brief overview of the article that accompanies it.

The second thing I needed to add were 20 tags or keywords that represent the main points being conveyed throughout the article. I'm learning more and more about how using keywords can make a big difference in your success to increase views of your article on social media. Toward that end, it's exciting to see all the changes being incorporated into our approach to improve and expand the impact and availability of grants.

Day 7: Tuesday

♟ Sue, Executive Office Manager

Podcast and Website: I was involved in filming and served as the virtual green room for the guests. Video clips were also filmed on this day during filming.

I supervised Chris and Pushpendra because Libby was filming. They continued working on the GrantWatch homepage, making improvements.

🎯 Aaron, Strategic Consultant

Using the content creation strategy provided by the team led by Nikita and Lori, Andre learned to script and set up content creation. We filmed numerous podcasts and hours' worth of short-form content and ads.

Although this can be a draining experience for beginners, after some practice and coaching, Libby performed phenomenally, producing short-form content incredibly efficiently by the end of the day.

📊 Nikita, Data Analyst / Media Manager

Today was a long day! I ended up working overtime to ensure we hit critical milestones. Picking up where we left off yesterday, I teamed up with Chris again, and together we launched two brand-new pages: one for *Funding Sources* and another for *Recipient Types*.

We also made several key updates across the site, including improving the chat box functionality and refining the layout of the "Create an Account" section on the homepage. After some focused effort, I finally wrapped up the research and updates for all the meta descriptions - another major task checked off the list.

One ongoing issue remains: the search filter on the homepage still isn't functioning correctly. It's clear the developers are feeling stretched thin, but we managed to rally them to push through and make progress before calling it a day.

All in all, it was an intense but productive day.

💻 Chris, Web Developer

Categories Page Layout: Today, I worked on the category pages. I created a new layout for the list of categories we use across the site. This list shows the different types of grants we offer. The new layout is simpler and easier to understand. It also works better on mobile devices. I made sure it can be reused on other pages that show categories.

💡 Pamela, Customer Support Specialist

Today, I wasn't involved. The meeting was during my break, and I was working on customer service tasks. I'm excited to see the changes. It seems like we got more chats today. I wonder if we are tracking engagement and if the new home page is attracting more interest. I hope so.

🜨 Danika, Grant Support Specialist – Collaboration:

Watching our contributions come to life has been exciting. Today, Libby was filming, and I am excited to see if she used the reel ideas that Lori, Nikita, and I had worked on earlier. It was rewarding to see our brainstorming directly influence the next steps.

✍ Lori, Editor and Media Manager

The logo was revised to be brighter. I updated the logo on both Pinterest and Twitter. I also collaborated with Adrian to develop a new five-image carousel layout for every article on Instagram, which we're testing as a more engaging visual format.

🎨 Adrian, Graphic Artist

It was the routine where I needed to go back and find the images to edit. It was a long process, as I previously wrote. There are many to get through, and it would be a process that requires going through all the images I have ready to make ready-to-publish. Besides that, I needed to redo the chat image for the website. No reason to make a GIF anymore, it'll be a static image. It was nice to remember the process, but the meeting described it as too old-fashioned. So, I made a new thing and sent it on its way.

🎥 Andre, Videographer

I was shown how to write scripts designed for teleprompters, including structuring hooks, reiteration, main content, and CTAs (call to action) to keep things concise and engaging. For example, say, type a word below, and I will send you a link to something. That creates engagement.

I'm getting faster at identifying what needs to be said and how to keep it engaging, concise, and natural on camera. It felt like a real step forward in crafting effective short-form scripts.

✉️ David, Email Marketing Consultant

I have no comments for today, as I have collected over 3,000 lines of data to be uploaded to different audiences. I isolated myself from the Team chat to avoid making any mistakes. Sometimes I do need to focus on numbers and formulas.

💬 Jeff, Writer

And It's a Wrap: So, another story (article) is 'put to bed.' It's always a great feeling when I literally get closure on an article I've spent a good amount of time creating. My goal is for my article(s) to provide a small but significant source of information. I hope it will help people find grants and boost our site, benefiting the company's overall goals.

On the technical front, the loss of Skype as our primary internal communication platform necessitated a migration to a different platform. That platform turns out to be called Teams. It has a few little quirks, but generally seems comparable to what Skype used to be. The biggest relief (for me) was that all our Chats transferred over to the Teams app. I don't know how that happened, but I'm certainly glad we didn't have to lose our Chat messages, since I use them to add notes for myself and track the posts I have made as part of our overall social media strategy.

Day 8: Wednesday

♟ Sue, Executive Office Manager

Zoom meeting: Today began with more website updates and changes, followed by a review of all social media accounts. Aaron had tons of excellent tips and ideas for promoting the website's brand through fonts, colors, and images. Today, I accomplished a tremendous amount of work on social media.

🎯 Aaron, Strategic Consultant

AI Developer Bolt integration: We continued website updates and social network updates while working closely with experienced staff, such as Nikita. We have started implementing changes to improve efficiency and boost revenue on the new and improved site. After these changes, the public portrayal of GrantWatch is entirely more professional.

📊 Nikita, Data Analyst / Media Manager

Halfway through the week, I'm genuinely impressed by how much progress we've made in such a short time. Still, today came with its own challenges - both emotional and operational.

One of my colleagues has been feeling left out of the renovation process, expressing that everyone else seems essential while they feel sidelined. With Sue overwhelmed and the rest of the team stretched thin, I proposed a side project that aligns with their strengths and won't interfere with their regular duties. It felt good to offer a solution that could bring them back into the fold - one small resolution achieved!

Chris, however, is clearly running on fumes. His energy and pace today were noticeably down from earlier in the week, and while I understand exhaustion, it's frustrating to see momentum slip just as we near the finish line. Missed details and delays are creeping in, and it's hard not to feel the pressure.

We had a team meeting focused on social media strategy, led by Aaron, our social media guru. I was happy to hear that the analytics I've been working on are now being factored into our strategy - it's validating to see that the work is making an impact. As part of that effort, we're also refreshing our social media banners to better align with the new site's updated look.

That said, there are still lingering glitches across the site, and with our dev team clearly overwhelmed, reporting them often feels like shouting into the void. It's disheartening.

During the meeting, Libby mentioned the need for a site index - fortunately, I'd already proactively started one! It turned out to be exactly what we needed, and it felt good to be one step ahead. Of course, the reality hit quickly: over 100 pages now need to be reviewed and revised. I'm excited for the challenge, but I can't say the developers will share my enthusiasm.

By the end of the day, feeling a bit defeated by the lack of progress on the tech side, I shifted my focus. I joined the support team and helped clear the backlog of difficult emails in the inbox. Oddly enough, the structure and clarity of support work brought me a sense of calm and accomplishment. Sometimes, helping people directly is the best reminder of why we do this in the first place.

▇ Chris, Web Developer

Foundation Directory Page: I focused on the foundation directory today. This page shows what different funders have given and supported. I updated the layout and changed the styles to match our new design. The page now looks more organized, and it's easier to scan the list of funders. I made sure it uses Bootstrap 5 just like the other pages.

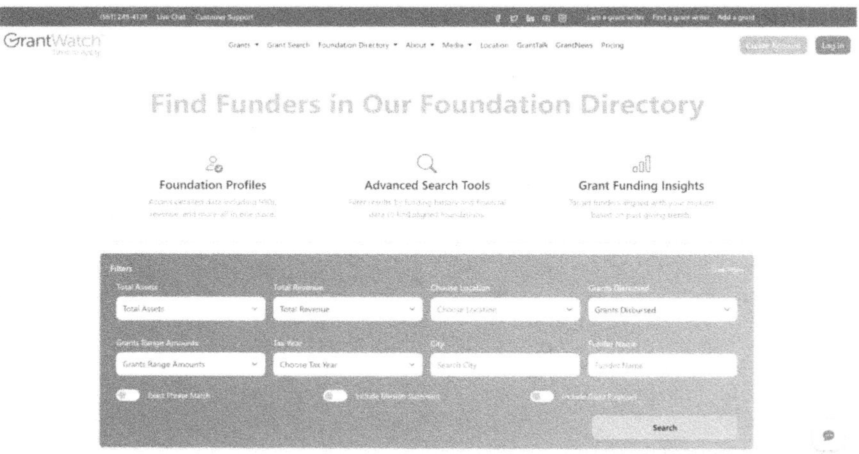

♀ Pamela, Customer Support Specialist

More changes are coming along. Glad we are making it clearer to the public that we only display verified grants. It appears that I am to help validate the URLs on the resource page section, which will add more value to the site.

The resource page is so important. Our clients are constantly looking for resources and assistance with the grant process. The more of a resource we can be, the better.

◔ Danika, Grant Support Specialist

Paid User Experience: I felt very positive and productive, excited by the idea that improving the user experience will also increase revenue. I suggested changes for the grant detail page, including making the "Apply" and "Hide Grant" features more visible. I was thrilled that my suggestions inspired the team. We also discussed highlighting the multi-user feature more prominently and refining the pricing page.

✍ Lori, Editor and Media Manager

I had started watching instructional videos on Metricool to better understand its features. I also looked for my working document, which we called our SOP (Standard Operating Procedure) for social media posting, but couldn't find it. I may have accidentally deleted it. Now I am starting from scratch with all the new methods we are implementing day by day.

I spent more time working closely with Adrian to finalize the new Instagram carousel images. I successfully posted our first carousel after learning how to upload multiple pages in a single post. The process was straightforward, and I'm really enjoying the new format. I'm eager to see how it performs and already have several questions as we move forward.

🎨 Adrian, Graphic Artist

I created a new version of the Facebook banner as well as the other social media. It was on short notice, so the edits had to wait until I had the banner up and ready to upload. I eventually finished making the banner for their separate websites. Off to make the edits again, then proceed to the article images and the social media images. I have a full schedule today. The looming deadlines of the new images are coming; I'll have to plan out how I'll keep everything in order. So much to keep in mind.

🎥 Andre, Videographer

I began applying the new techniques using OpusClip, filming, and framing that were recently introduced to me. I completed the video by combining my own experience with the newly learned tools and programs, creating a balanced approach that reflects both familiarity and growth.

✉ David, Email Marketing Consultant

Just continued following our general Team chat, now on MS Teams, wondering how and when I could get on any project, and at the same time, doing the best to keep on schedule on Mailchimp.

🧠 Jeff, Writer

Getting Started in Earnest: To start searching for grants, I must decide which category is most relevant. The theme was originally intended to be Adult-related sports and recreation. But I soon discovered that there are very few grants specifically for adults. However, there are a good number of grants relating to Community Recreation/Activities, so I'll need to slightly modify the title to reflect that. Now I'm in a position to begin my search!

We now seem to be getting into the meat of the project. We are approaching it from different perspectives. The call center gang wants to make sure everything is as easy as possible for potential subscribers. They need to get a good sense of what we're all about to decide whether to subscribe. For me, it's a lot simpler. I just need grant information to be readily available (by category).

Day 9: Thursday

♟ Sue, Executive Office Manager

Changes! We reviewed the changes made the day before and how to improve the homepage and other pages, even more. Faced some challenges getting everyone on board with the purpose of our meetings. Discussed a lot about chats, customer service, and increasing sales. Went on to social images, trying to decide between AI-created vs. human images. The meeting went on to discuss saves, calendars, and apply buttons in the grants.

◎ Aaron, Strategic Consultant

Growth Conversation: We worked through the website, updated our social media images to high res photos that match our overall developed strategy and ended the day with a discussion with Libby and Ellisa about effective LinkedIn outreach, her role within GrantWatch, the growth ideas I have for the future of the company, and how we can expand using modern technologies and innovation while maintaining the current business structure and model.

📊 Nikita, Data Analyst / Media Manager

Today has been frustrating. Our developer isn't feeling well, and without enthusiastic development support, progress has slowed to a crawl - right when we need it most. I've been uncovering major errors on the site, and while I've shared them with Sue, we're often stuck in a holding pattern. What we view as urgent isn't always treated as such by the dev team, and that disconnect is worrying. I'm genuinely concerned about how these issues will impact our users; all I want is a seamless, professional experience for our customers.

This whole situation has deepened my appreciation for just how critical a dependable, responsive developer is to a digital project.

During today's meeting, I worked with Libby and Aaron to plan updates for the "Grant Detail" page. I'm genuinely excited about the changes we mapped out, but unfortunately, they've joined a long queue of pending tasks. Without a developer to implement them, they'll have to wait.

Chris is sick, projects are stalling, and I can't push any harder. So, to regain a sense of focus, I turned my attention back to the support inbox - it's become my anchor lately. The clarity of solving specific customer issues, one at a time, brings a small but steady sense of progress.

Then I got a call from Elissa - a meeting I had completely forgotten about. We discussed how best to utilize her assets moving forward, and I'm excited about what she can contribute. A bit of light in an otherwise slow-moving day.

Later, Sue called me to brainstorm how we could make our team meetings more efficient - through recordings or recaps. For once, I didn't have an immediate solution, which is rare for me. Still, I'm hopeful that with a fresh perspective tomorrow, something will click.

Here's to a better Friday.

📕 Chris, Web Developer

Filters and Location Page: I returned to the homepage filters and made additional changes to improve their appearance and functionality. After that, I started working on the "All Locations" page. This page lists all the places where grants are available. I cleaned up the layout and began switching it over to Bootstrap 5. It still needs a bit more work, but it's looking better already.

💡 Pamela, Customer Support Specialist

Libby asked us to find an emoji to identify our daily entry in the book. Choosing an emoji for the book is fun yet so hard.

I know I have had many light bulb moments, so that is what I chose. Looking forward to further optimizing the search. Have some exciting plans for the resource pages and how-to videos.

◌ Danika, Grant Support Specialist

Personal Highlight: Today, we restructured our approach to a full social media plan. I felt really great about the direction the team was taking. At Lori's request, I also helped Adrian brainstorm solutions to some image design issues he was facing, which felt like a valuable collaboration.

I quoted a very large multi-user account today, proof that the site's improvements are already making a real impact. I spoke to Sue and reinforced the importance of restructuring our multi-user options. It was very insightful to learn that a previous partnership between grants and SNPO had ended, opening new possibilities for us to strengthen multi-user offerings. Most of these users operate with budgets between $4,000 and $10,000. I asked probing questions to understand their needs and expectations. I am excited to continue exploring how we can further grow these opportunities.

✍ Lori, Editor and Media Manager

I continued watching Metricool tutorials and posted another Instagram carousel. I had planned to post a third, but encountered an error that prevented it. I also wrote and scheduled my first post using Metricool, which is set to go live Friday morning.

This test will help determine whether Metricool is a suitable tool for transferring our full posting calendar.

🎨 Adrian, Graphic Artist

Banner day again. I needed to redo the social media banners, going through a lengthy process of finding the right image that conveyed the website's theme and having the woman in the post face away from the viewer. I managed to strike a balance that they found acceptable. I'll have to once again make an emphasis. Making the new banner was very lengthy. Every detail needs to be acceptable and not look weird. I used the composite method to create a highly specific image and to modify the elements around it. In the end, I received an A+ on my work. Not bad. Always nice to get an image approved after so many changes requested.

🎥 Andre, Videographer

After participating in a brainstorming session with Aaron and Libby, I received feedback on the framing and thumbnails to make them more engaging.

I found an effective way to encompass these new ideas. I believe the new direction will lead to stronger results, as there's now a clearer vision for creating ads and reels that align with our goals.

✉ David, Email Marketing Consultant

This day I finally upgraded my VPN from Basic Free to a full paid Subscription, as it was the right moment to do, I needed to log on our Website faster than usual, as those changes and task regarding them needed a better work around in my case, avoiding to switch back and forth with a bad VPN was taking some time, also it was an improvement for one of my daily tasks that is looking for address on Data Mining.

🧠 Jeff, Writer

Finding the Grants People Will Want: It may sound like an easy task to pick out grants from the selected category. But then, you may not yet have searched through the THOUSANDS of grants to choose from! Of course, I can narrow the field dramatically once I filter the list by category, but each category has hundreds - some with thousands - of grants once that filter has been applied. Then it becomes a matter of choosing from the many filters available on the GrantWatch site to narrow the field.

As far as the staff goes, we have the opportunity to be very involved in discussing which changes and/or additions might be included in the final site redesign. Since I'm not generally involved with many specific, site-related needs, it's still great to hear from the others about which changes are most needed and HOW best to incorporate them into the new design.

Day 10: Friday

♟ Sue, Executive Office Manager

Website Down! It would have been nice to start a Friday without the website being down. The website was fixed and is back up and running. The best part of today is that Pushpendra fixed all the issues with the crons and emails, and everything is running smoothly. So, this is a nice way to end a Friday. The Zoom call continued with Libby, Lani, and Aaron. Then continued with Chris, who did a superb job updating the website with changes from Libby and Nikita.

◎ Aaron, Strategic Consultant

The team continued work on the site; we resolved some difficulties with social media posts and software, clarified expected timelines with the graphic and content creation departments, and ended the day with a call with Elana about grant research and editing operations and how we can develop software to improve them. Chris and Nikita worked past my time on continuing site improvements.

📊 Nikita, Data Analyst / Media Manager

Today was a short day. I was logged out by the system after less than 2 hours because I reached my weekly hour limit. Since Libby asked me to work on Sunday and start early on Tuesday, I anticipated this and gave both her and Sue a heads-up yesterday. I will see everyone next week.

Honestly, I don't mind taking a break. It's been a productive and intense week, and I've put in strong work. Still, I can't help but feel a little disappointed. There's so much still outstanding, and it's tough to step away when I know how much needs to be done.

Plot twist: After about 20 minutes, I was called back in to wrap up a few remaining tasks - always nice to feel needed! I teamed up with Libby and Chris to finalize the coding for the GrantWatch page, which went smoothly. I'll be coming in on Sunday to get a head start on the next set of tasks before the rest of the team arrives on Monday.

📱 Chris, Web Developer

Pricing and Payment Pages: I worked on two important pages today. First, I updated the pricing page to use a newer Bootstrap version and made small design changes to clarify it. Then I worked on the payment page to improve the layout and user flow. We had a team call, and everyone felt good about how these two pages turned out. The feedback was positive, and I'm glad we're moving in the right direction.

💡 Pamela, Customer Support Specialist

Site is down.... wonder what's going on. It lasted only a minute or two. Hopefully, it is for more progress. The home page looks great, but I think it could still use some tweaking of the font size and color. The new pricing page looks good, too. Again, I think with some slight formatting changes, it will be even better. Hopefully, the others will agree with some of my suggestions. But I think this is getting even better for clients.

⭕ Danika, Grant Support Specialist

Reflection: Friday, what a week! Today was all about catching up with my admin tasks. However, I can clearly see our user experience has already improved. I connected with more qualified users today, which felt incredibly rewarding.

Today, I also had the chance to get to know Elissa better. She is very easy to talk to and clearly a hard worker. I am excited to see how she will help Libby refine and grow GrantWatch.

Every time I help a nonprofit that serves the homeless or those in need of medical care, I help people all over the world, and that is my favorite part about working here. I am grateful to be even a small part of the reason these nonprofits can thrive.

As we move into the next 10 days, there is an incredible sense of momentum as the team's innovative ideas take shape. I can see we are aligned as a group, now more than ever.

The future is bright, and I am excited to be part of this journey.

✍ Lori, Editor and Media Manager

Friday brought a mix of progress and complications. I had scheduled three social media posts the previous day using Metricool.

However, I encountered an issue: many of our posts require a direct article link, and those links aren't available until the content is published in WordPress. This means I must go back into each post after publication to manually insert the link. While Metricool is fun to use, this process adds more steps rather than saving time.

Additionally, I wasn't able to schedule posts to X (formerly Twitter) despite having previously purchased access for $7-$9, which included X ad functionality. This feature still isn't working. I manually added the article link to each of the three test posts. Platform results varied:

Pinterest doesn't allow edits to posts uploaded with Metricool; you'll need to start over and reschedule.

LinkedIn failed to load the post image, so I had to delete and repost it manually. I wrote to Metricool, and they quickly fixed the preset.

Facebook functioned without any issues.

I made a few user errors as well: I forgot to add a title to the Pinterest post, though I thought I had, so I'll double-check next time. I also spent time resolving timing errors on Pinterest and correcting a post that initially included the wrong link.

On the technical side, there appears to be no option to edit a post once it has been published on Metricool, unless there's a workaround I haven't found yet. One persistent challenge remains: because our articles are written in WordPress and don't generate URLs until publication, I can't add the links to posts scheduled in advance. Finding a solution to this will be essential for streamlining our workflow.

🎨 Adrian, Graphic Artist

I was advised during the Zoom meeting that the images needed to look more inviting to the layperson, in terms of visual engagement. They reiterated that the text needs to be bold yet brief, and worded to suggest availability or urgency in finding grants. They also posed using a different image to be more inviting and cuter. It was about a dog. I found a cuter dog; I can tell you that. That's unfair; all dogs are precious, but we needed a dog to look into the camera.

I succeeded in that task. I had a dog once. Or twice. I am familiar with dogs, though I'm not sure that having owned one back then is a prerequisite for looking for dog pictures online. I'll say no. Also, the directive changed. Lengthy? No, I need to make them brief, big, and bold. Frustrating how I'll need to go through them again. At least he copped to the change in his story, but that still doesn't change the fact that the work I did needed to be negated. Oh well, back to all the images. Again.

🎥 Andre, Videographer

Continued progress on deliverables while adapting to evolving expectations and maintaining a high level of attention to detail while editing video.

✉ David, Email Marketing Consultant

This was not a good day, at least on the first hours as our Website was down, this meant a delay on my daily chores, but to make things worse, I logged in late for our Zoom meeting, I was completely lost in the language of the meeting as at that moment our developers were on their language and skills and I was not aware on their input for Website, sometimes on our meetings I am lost when developers are involved and I try to follow up, but it is very hard, however I felt that we are moving in the right direction, and after seeing what is being accomplished it is a reality.

🧠 Jeff, Writer

Another Article is Put to Bed: Once again, it's a great feeling of satisfaction - together with a little bit of relief - to be able to complete and submit another article to be published. I take great pride in the finished product, so while it needs to be both informative and interesting, I also want to do as much as possible to ensure it is accurately written with few, if any, corrections.

As for the team, it was great to see the continued progress on the site and everyone's efforts to make it as clear and easy to read as possible.

Day 10.5: Sunday

📊 Nikita, Data Analyst / Media Manager

Today, I got access to a new program to help revamp our email newsletters, which is super exciting! I spent a good chunk of time perfecting the designs, only to hit a wall when it came time to implement them. Turns out, coding for emails isn't quite as smooth as chatting with an AI.

One frustrating lesson I quickly learned: just because something looks great in one browser doesn't mean it'll behave the same in others or on different devices! Thankfully, Push has offered to guide me through the process tomorrow. Fingers crossed that things start to make a bit more sense with some expert help!

Day 11: Monday

🏆 Sue, Executive Office Manager

New Beginnings: Kicking off Monday with my first task was genuinely exciting. The updated page I use to send out the daily emails featuring 25 of the newest grants looked absolutely beautiful. What a refreshing and welcome improvement.

Our morning meeting began with a team review of the new TikTok short videos that Andre filmed. We each shared feedback on how to enhance and fine-tune them. The highlight of the meeting, however, was the preview of the newly designed website pages. It's energizing to see how these improvements can boost sales, reduce subscriber issues, and empower our staff to generate more business.

We wrapped up the session with Chris, who resolved login and password issues for both free and paid members, another important step toward smoother user experiences.

🎯 Aaron, Strategic Consultant

Team input is invaluable for noticing details and creating a final product. We noticed this as the day started with a team meeting and by watching the short-form clips Andre made for Social Media. Everyone contributed their input and improvements to ensure a high-quality, professional product was produced. Andre, being easy to work with, took the edits in stride as he navigated managing a new system. He is definitely putting in effort to rise to the occasion.

Social Media Analytics from the first weeks alone have shown results, with a 400%+ increase in organic Instagram engagement compared to posts before the implementation of our improved social media strategy, without a single dollar of ad spend.

Throughout the day, we met with Libby, Chris, Nikita, & Sue to discuss our vital site renovations. It's a process, with the team working incredibly hard, even overtime, to accomplish the goals. As the data showed, even within a week, we already had significant site improvement and SEO results. Expanding our lead of Grants.gov and any "competitors" by an abnormal margin for such a short period of time.

I broke away from the team to develop a Facebook ad campaign, Implementing Marketing strategies and drawing on expertise I've learned over my career, including analyzing publicly available data and AI to develop a test campaign structure with custom scripts and CTAs. The constructed campaign was sent to Adrian for development, and we hope to implement the strategy this week!

These changes are big, and the team is learning to adjust. We are making incredible strides necessary for improved growth across all fronts and are already seeing astronomical results in such a short period of time. I truly appreciate working with such a positive and dedicated team whose expertise is being properly utilized in development, and the work ethic makes such large changes possible!

📊 Nikita, Data Analyst / Media Manager

I started work early today, hoping to learn from Push and finally get a handle on the newsletter coding issues. Unfortunately, he was unavailable again. It's incredibly frustrating not to have an available web developer, especially when that role is so vital at GrantWatch. With every issue we fix, five new ones seem to appear elsewhere. Honestly, I'd sacrifice two months of my salary just to have a dependable dev on board.

In the meantime, I shifted gears and worked with Chris to help implement some quick changes Libby needed. Between those updates, I tackled the email inbox to reduce the Monday support load. Hopefully, this gave the support team a head start so they could focus on the important stuff once their day began, allowing me to focus on mine without them asking for help.

Later, I tried using Bolt again to redesign the newsletter. I specifically asked it to generate code that works across all platforms and devices, but the output failed again. Still, I'm proud I'm not giving up, I'm actively thinking of solutions, even if they aren't all working yet. I've learnt not to rely on Push.

Then came the big issue of the day: the login process. Sue and I ended up in a tense debate over how it works. Right now, a non-paying user sees "Partial Successful Login," while a paying user sees "Successful Login."

The problem? Most of our paying users don't know they need to log out before logging in, or forget their passwords, and end up canceling, largely because the system doesn't work well for them.

When I showed evidence of this pattern, we dug deeper and discovered something alarming: if a non-paying user ever logs out, they can't log in again. Ever. That's a huge loss in potential customers and revenue. We brought it to Chris and Libby, and Chris proposed that everyone be given a password by default.

We were nearly done, just needed to update the pop-ups, when Sue decided against the idea. Libby then had Chris revert the whole update. So, we had to pivot again. The new rule? Non-paying members can't have, create, or be issued a password. Tomorrow will be a new day and a new challenge to be tackled.

🖥 Chris, Web Developer

Fixing a Long-Standing Bug: I started the day by making a few updates to the pricing page. After that, I designed a new thank-you page that users see after completing a payment. While I was in the middle of working on other pages, Nikita found a bug on the login page.

The issue was that non-paid members were being asked for a password, even though they never set one during signup. I had a meeting with Nikita and Sue to talk about how to fix it.

At first, we thought the best solution was to force all users to create a password, but later we realized there were other signup popups on the site that didn't follow that logic. After talking with Libby, we decided to undo that change and instead fix the bug directly. I finally fixed it, even though it kept me sitting still for hours. I'm glad that part is now solved.

💡 Pamela, Customer Support Specialist

We had another meeting today. It looks like the pricing page will have some changes. That's great. The page is, of course, so important. Also made some progress on pricing for enterprise accounts. This is huge. This can mean a big increase in the number of nonprofits we serve.

🌑 Danika, Grant Support Specialist

New videos were presented today, and Libby was amazing! She came across as both friendly and knowledgeable. I'm excited to see how these videos help with engagement and conversion.

We talked about adding municipalities as a new seeker type, which I'm *very* excited about. Many municipalities do not realize they qualify as nonprofit equivalents, so adding this option could help them better identify themselves and find relevant funding.

We also discussed adding a green envelope icon for multi-user setup, similar to the one we use now for check payments.

Another key idea was making the multi-user option more visible on the pricing page to drive conversions.

Monday was a typically busy day, and while we didn't get to the pricing discussion from Friday, we made progress on other exciting fronts.

✍ Lori, Editor and Media Manager

I was able to use the Metricool system to schedule posts. I worked on scheduling Facebook, Instagram, LinkedIn, and Pinterest, but not X. It works well. I also spent a large chunk of my day studying analytics.

Aaron will go over these in more detail with me at some point, but I wanted to get a jump on the material. The information is straightforward and presented in easy-to-understand graphics. Nice. I also used some of my time working with Adrian on the images and the ad style for the new campaigns.

🎨 Adrian, Graphic Artist

I was tasked with creating a bunch of images for Aaron. They were Facebook Ads; he provided the guidelines, though obtaining them took a bit of time. I never received that email. I had to inquire about it. Throughout the day, I worked on the ads while also fulfilling my weekly duty of creating the newsletter. The work on the ads will go on to the next day; there's a lot to do. A very busy day. The plan is laid out, the day is set. A look into what my week will be like.

🎥 Andre, Videographer

I started adjusting my workflow, compositions, and content production using OpusClip. I started by exporting it as a video, then realized I could export it as an editable project so I could edit specific elements. I can then open it in Adobe Premiere Pro and precisely adjust the scale and position.

I developed a system for how I'm creating ads. It's become a reliable framework that I can apply to any campaign I work on.

✉️ David, Email Marketing Consultant

Day started with a Zoom meeting, we had to analyze some commercial videos and write our observations on each one, I found that my observations coincided almost perfectly with those from

Danika, she is one of the Super Girls as I call them, just energetic, on top of everything, fast and always like she had batteries as breakfast, Pamela is the other Super Girl, when they take over these meetings I just jump on the roller coaster. Yesterday I waited for some changes to Mail templates that delayed my regular schedule; it was a bit frustrating to be off track, but it was for the greater good, and the frustration faded.

🧠 Jeff, Writer

Company Systems Changes to Learn: The effort to tighten and improve our internal systems has been really interesting for me. Since I'm not as involved as some others in the day-to-day workings of the revenue side of the ball, it's very revealing to see just how much time and (ongoing) effort are needed if you want to get it right. From my side, it's great to see all the positive changes on our homepage. Hopefully, it will be easier to view, with a lot more info up front, so you get a better idea of the quality grant resources we can offer.

Day 12: Tuesday

♟ Sue, Executive Office Manager

Working the Magic: Today began with our daily Zoom call with Aaron, where we continued brainstorming effective solutions for social media platforms and developing targeted, useful ads. From there, it was on to daily operations, including investigating refund requests and assisting members with their grant searches.

Thankfully, the email system ran smoothly today, a welcome relief. I spent much of the day catching up after a week of meetings. We called Chris again to resolve a login issue for free members, and he handled it promptly and efficiently.

The rest of the day was dedicated to addressing emails and managing Multi-User accounts.

◎ Aaron, Strategic Consultant

Facebook Ads, the highly effective way for companies to reach their clientele in 2025, was my focus for Day 12. Effectively utilizing, testing, and launching a successful ad campaign can potentially lead to massive revenue increases for GrantWatch. After designing the structure, writing the scripts, cross-checking them for errors, and using Adrian's efficiently prepared graphics, I set up a test campaign for the ads.

The structure of this campaign will be to spread 50 clickable phrases with graphics and low ad spend to identify which ads achieve the highest conversion rate. After we identify which ads convert at the highest rates, we will focus ad spend solely on those ads and run a successful campaign targeting our clientele with the phrases they click, ultimately converting them into customers.

Another focus of the day was explaining the importance of our staff engaging with our followers on social media. Yesterday, our post had numerous accounts with 100k followers who organically engaged and requested to share it, yet we had no system in place to engage with them, potentially costing us 1M+ impressions! Again, we are speaking about an account that only two weeks ago had ZERO organic traffic, and now we are discussing collaboration with large accounts organically. This is a testament to the incredible adaptability and skill of the team led by Lori, Nikita, and Adrian in developing a new and improved social media strategy and its effective execution.

Nikita, Data Analyst / Media Manager

Since I'll be away for the next few days, I tried to wrap up as many unfinished tasks as I could. I also put together a clear to-do list for anyone stepping in to help supervise Chris on the development side; hopefully, it'll make things easier for them to pick up where I left off without feeling overwhelmed or lost. After that, I used the rest of my time to update the Excel sheet with new grants for Israel. Even though I've done my best to prepare, I know I'll still be worrying while I'm away about how things are moving along.

📲 Chris, Web Developer

Gaining Momentum: Today was a really productive day. I worked on the "About Us", "Testimonials", "On The Road", "Queen of Grants" book page, and "Contact Us" pages. I've started to gain real momentum and completed all five pages in one day. Each page now uses our new Bootstrap 5 design, and they all feel much more modern and cleaner.

We also had another team call, during which I shared my progress with everyone. It felt good to walk them through what I've been working on. The feedback was positive and encouraging. Everything is really starting to come together, and I'm feeling even more excited to see the final version of the site when all the pages are done. We're definitely on the right track!

💡 Pamela, Customer Support Specialist

Looks like some of those interior pages are coming along. I do like the idea of having our grants stand out more on our home page. I guess we will see what happens. Glad to see our Instagram showing traction and wonder what the ads team will come up with.

◎ Danika, Grant Support Specialist

The vision was starting to come together, and I was genuinely thrilled with the direction of the new user experience. Nikita is doing an excellent job of project-managing the changes we've discussed as a team.

Lori and Nikita also worked on restructuring the social media plan to give it a more modern, strategic direction, with some great input from Aaron. It's exciting to see these ideas come to life.

✍ Lori, Editor and Media Manager

Another day working with Metricool, and I'm learning a lot through trial and error! While I ran into some posting issues, it's giving me a deeper understanding of how the platform behaves.

The Instagram error message taught me the importance of giving longer posts extra buffer time. Facebook gave a false positive on a successful post, but that's another useful clue as we troubleshoot.

Pinterest worked perfectly, love how seamless it is there! I also responded to several comments from Monday's post. It's always rewarding to engage with our audience.

🎨 Adrian, Graphic Artist

Much like yesterday, I created the images dictated by the Google Doc sheet I was assigned previously. I was able to get through that, but I had to spend extra time on it to have it ready for presentation. Between that, I needed to help create images for Asana to catch up on the images I needed to complete. The new process takes a bit longer than it did originally, but from the sounds of it, it's working. Good stuff, really good stuff, I'll say. I also started making the various logos for different territories. That is taking a good bit of time as well. Most things seem to take time. That's a theme here, judging by the previous entries. That's work, though, especially for those who desire fast processes and close deadlines.

🎥 Andre, Videographer

Today moved quickly– because it had to. The clock became my rival, and I was a soldier battling against it.

The ads were my mission– clean, fast, exact. Face smoothing came first, a balance between realism and refinement. No detail escaped me; every wrinkle softened, every imperfection erased. The final edits unfolded like dominoes, thanks to the Opus software.

Something happened today. Something I didn't expect, Libby's words ignited something within me.

A flame. I looked back at my previous journal entries from earlier days, and I rewrote them with more personality.

Because Libby had reminded me that we don't just record history—we write it with a passion befitting the great grant writers.

✉ David, Email Marketing Consultant

Today we had an early Zoom meeting, as soon as it started, I realized the main theme was about social media, but not the phrase we usually hear in movies or TV shows; instead, it was hardcore social media, metrics, conversions, shifting policies, publicity investing, etc. I can resume what I understood with the same ability I have for a menu in Cantonese; I know what I'm eating just by name...No other words. Slowly, our meeting turned on TikTok, and then I knew I was completely lost. Just before meeting ended, we all congratulated Nikita on her upcoming birthday, she is one of our oldest team members, not on age but in years working for GW, as usual, I wondered how she does her work, she lives in Brisbane,

Australia and her hours are crazy, soon my day started to be the same, as Mailchimp was waiting for me.

🗣 Jeff, Writer - Catching Up to the Pack

I came into the project a little later than most, so I did some catching up.

 In the meantime, we started out the morning with a general staff meeting to review just some of the major improvements being made to our website. It was really eye-opening for me to gain more of an understanding of just how much time and energy is needed to ensure that potential subscribers have their questions answered, are given the proper direction to check out the site themselves, and then, hopefully, get them formally signed on as a subscriber to our site to gain full access to the amazing set of tools and resources available to them!

Day 13: Wednesday

⚱ Sue, Executive Office Manager

It's a Wonderful Day in the Neighborhood: We kicked off the day on a high note with a productive Zoom meeting covering several exciting updates. We fine-tuned the Grant Detail page, reviewed the new button designs, and discussed ways to enhance the visibility of the Keyword Search Box. We also considered adding explanatory text to let users know they can enter a GrantWatch ID directly into the search field for quick access.

Later, I got together with Pushpendra to address long-standing issues on the Multi-User quote pages and the Add Check page, both of which are now resolved.

We wrapped up the meeting by reviewing the day's priorities for Aaron and Chris. Overall, it was a very positive and productive day, with everyone staying focused and making meaningful progress toward our goals.

🎯 Aaron, Strategic Consultant

Wednesday started with social media analytics, showing results from our social media having gained a great following from our posts, and showing the trends across socials all going up!

The rest of the day was spent developing and deploying our Facebook ad campaign, which is spread across 4 sections and 57 posts. Although generally we would explore a much longer campaign, due to the time sensitivity we are running an "express" strategy where we will find the best performing ads and run them

10X. If successful, this can lead to massive sales increases for our site.

🖳 Chris, Web Developer

Big Ideas and Big Pages: I kicked off the day with a quick and energizing call with Yaffa to talk about something really exciting: developing a grant extraction tool powered by AI. We're exploring how to use deep research features in AI models to help us grow our grant database much faster. It's a huge opportunity, and the possibilities are exciting. After the call, I spent some time researching the best AI models for the job and shared my findings with Libby. I had only set aside an hour for this research, so once that was done, I jumped right back into the frontend work.

I made progress on a few smaller pages before diving into one of the most important parts of the site: the grant-details page. This page is massive, with thousands of lines of code, so I had to take a focused and careful approach. I broke it into manageable sections and was able to finish most of them today. I saved the rest for tomorrow so I can approach it with a fresh mind.

Before ending the day, we had a team meeting to go over some ideas for improving the homepage. The goal is to create a version that not only looks great but also converts better. Everyone contributed helpful suggestions, and the energy around this redesign is really strong. I'm feeling very motivated and excited about the direction we're heading. The site is really starting to transform!

💡 Pamela, Customer Support Specialist

Today, we discussed changing multi-user accounts and adding an affiliate program. It will be interesting to see what happens. These larger organizations could really benefit from our services. I am wondering which affiliate platform we will use.

🜨 Danika, Grant Support Specialist

Today, I filled in for Nikita and worked with Chris on the "Libby Approved" changes Nikita provided. These changes included updates to both the grant detail page and the home page. It's rewarding to see these visual and functional changes taking shape.

Libby also approved a new subcategory requested by Lani to help the users find relevant grants. "Medical research would be its own category or a sub of a sub."

Later in the day, we discussed pricing and subscription options in more detail. Here are some notes from Libby's EOD pricing discussion (5/14):

Enterprise "Library" Accounts

$250 setup fee

Simultaneous users purchased in blocks of 100

Chris and Push will review how to prevent scrapers from misusing the login

Important: Confirm that seekers logging in via the enterprise account are validated users

Affiliate Program

Seekers sign up independently

Libby contributes 5% back to the affiliate as a thank-you, or it can be passed along as an extra discount to the subscriber

We're gaining momentum. More to come!

✍ Lori, Editor and Media Manager

Testing day! I scheduled posts across Pinterest, Facebook, and Instagram. Aaron let me know that the LinkedIn issue might be resolved, so I jumped right in to test it. Instagram still struggles with long posts, but I had a breakthrough: even when Metricool shows an error, the post may still publish after a short delay. That's great news and definitely something to factor into future scheduling. The LinkedIn image issue is still lingering, but I'm zeroing in on the fix. Every test gets us closer to smoother operations!

🎨 Adrian, Graphic Artist

The day was mostly spent creating and fixing logos for the various territories. While initially I went about creating them based on what I could approximate the staff wanted, it is best to look at past efforts to get an overall idea of the direction. So I may have left the initial logo designs up on Dropbox, designs I uploaded before I got a better understanding of the direction. My mistake. While I was remaking them, I got a summons; it looked like they saw. Fair enough, off to the Zoom meeting I go. It didn't help one bit that Dropbox decided to be obstinate just as I tried to upload. Besides the design and composition they wanted changed, they also pointed out a minor misspelling.

Whether it be the truncated nature of some of these tasks, making errors like this occur, or I may have conflated a different word due to a wandering mind, I'll take accountability for not catching it, regardless. Not a very eventful day if that's what I'm mulling about, all things considered.

🎥 Andre, Videographer

I made fixes to the ads, then finalized a GrantTalk episode for review. I sent it off and waited.

I needed the YouTube password. I asked.

No response, only clues. The clues only hinted at the truth.

Dropbox gave me the same indifference, mockingly unresponsive every time I clicked refresh.

Silence, thick and indifferent.

So I searched through old messages, like an archaeologist analyzing forgotten scrolls. And then– there it was.

The password.

Not just a string of characters but a key to the gate of YouTube. I uploaded the video and began editing more ads, the start of another journey in my video editing.

✉ David, Email Marketing Consultant

As we started on out early Zoom meeting, soon I realized that the team was revising edits on our Web and I had some concerns on the banner where the YouTube channel is displayed, fortunately I was not the only voice of concern regarding this image, later on, Push, our developer Guru, told us he would start on the email templates, as this is my main area I was cautious to ask on a delivery date so I could test them, later on mid-day I participated for the first time on a MailChimp Webinar, I would love to discuss everything on which we could improve in that area, will try to look for an opportunity because I don't want to distract our team leaders on the subject, just to maximize our consultant's few available days with us.

🧠 Jeff, Writer

Delving More into social media: So, Sue hosted our chat gathering this morning. It's been helpful being able to check in with the rest of the staff and continue to delve into the mysteries of social media. Libby got this guy, Aaron, to help us fortify our social media structure, and it certainly sounds like we're already seeing some good results. I may not be the most social media-savvy guy around, but I do have a general understanding of what input is needed to ensure that social media advertising and marketing efforts are fruitful.

According to Aaron, we're already seeing results that are above and beyond expectations. Even though my role in this is relatively minor, it's good to be part of a strategy that gives you tangible results!

Day 14: Thursday

♟ Sue, Executive Office Manager

We began today's Zoom call by having Aaron review the current campaigns and their performance. He noted that it may take several days to see meaningful changes in engagement. Since his time with us is limited, he's testing a range of small, strategic adjustments, such as swapping images and targeting different audiences, to determine what resonates best. In short, he's running a wide variety of campaign tests to identify the most effective approaches.

Next, we revisited the homepage redesign. While we initially thought it was close to perfect, we're realizing it still needs some refining. We're adjusting the layout to bring the most important features front and center. On a positive note, the mobile version of the homepage looks stunning, truly the best it's ever been.

Later in the call, Aaron gave us a helpful overview of social media strategies, particularly around TikTok and understanding algorithms to improve reach. We wrapped up the Zoom session with Libby, continuing our discussion of improvements to the homepage.

🎯 Aaron, Strategic Consultant

Engagement on the site was lower than usual. We had a meeting to address the situation, discuss the variables, and deliver potential solutions. We ended up returning to some previous site features while maintaining the new design. We cannot go back to the old site; we have to make this one convert better than the previous one. Which we will do.

The entire team's input was helpful in addressing this situation and figuring out the issue at hand. We hope to see positive results. Lori mentioned this could be due to the waning intrigue in our GOAT articles after repeated use, and maybe we need another great article to boost engagement.

The rest of my day was focused on deploying our broad Facebook ad campaign and ensuring it was executed correctly. Although it takes time for Facebook campaigns to narrow down the correct audience, we saw positive results and early conversions already starting Thursday evening, a great sign!

💻 Chris, Web Developer

Fine-Tuning the Experience: Today, I continued refining the grant details page and made several changes to the homepage layout. We were moving components around; buttons, filters, and content sections, to create a more intuitive and user-friendly flow.

The team and I had a long and thoughtful discussion about placement and structure. It felt like piecing together a puzzle, making sure everything fits just right to guide users naturally. Every small adjustment made the experience smoother. It's exciting to see the homepage evolve this way.

💡 Pamela, Customer Support Specialist

It was an interesting meeting. I learned about Aaron's thinking process regarding launching a Facebook ads campaign geared toward educators and nonprofit executives. As we go along, we will continue to refine it.

◑ Danika, Grant Support Specialist

Iterations & Planning: Today, further refinements were made to the homepage. I remain hopeful it will align with our conversion requirements.

I caught up on the Support inbox and followed up on my multi-user pricing quotes.

In addition, I worked on an article due next week to maintain my two-month lead on article responsibilities.

✍ Lori, Editor and Media Manager

Today brought a win! I continued testing with Metricool and discovered the key to getting LinkedIn images to show up properly is changing a single display setting. Simple fix, big result! The posting speed still varies across platforms, but knowing the patterns helps a lot. Pinterest is lightning-fast, Facebook is consistent, and Instagram just needs a bit of patience. Each day, I'm gaining more insight and confidence using the platform. Excited to keep refining our process!

🎨 Adrian, Graphic Artist

A very regimented day, working on three different projects at once, having to make sure everything is consistent. And fixed. A lot of things to fix, again. Made me think a bit, the nature of working gets my mind wandering a bit, getting a bit of self-reflecting. I like to observe interactions and get a sense of the mood. I find that I really don't like prodding others, especially if they are inundated with work, especially nowadays with the transition into new strategies and workflows. By interacting with the others, I can get a good ballpark of what they are dealing with. We all have our limits on what we can do at once. As I get older, I find myself shouldering the weight of everything, making it lighter for others. An aspect of the day that I find is becoming more prevalent. Even when I start heading into my twilight years, I'll keep shouldering that weight for others. The world's heavy, living in it is accepting that heft, I suppose. Also, Photoshop decided to bug out on me; that was a bit annoying.

🎥 Andre, Videographer

The rhythm of the edit returned. I reopened the *GrantTalk* project, familiar timelines blinking like old companions. There was no fanfare - just the quiet discipline of refinement. I trimmed, adjusted, and smoothed, as one might tend to a garden no one sees bloom, but all enjoy in silence.

✉ David, Email Marketing Consultant

Today, we did not have a meeting, so I seized the opportunity to upload as much data to Mailchimp as I could while I waited for a Zoom call. At the end, I could upload all audiences, then a few minutes later, I realized some templates had changed, and for good, as colors were bold and modern. Later, after my regular hours ended, I decided to make a short video from yesterday's webinar, just a clip in which I presented a proposal to my CEO. She was already considering it; however, some additional information never hurts.

🧠 Jeff, Writer

The Start of a Promising Campaign: Now, getting into the main goal of identifying grants to include in the next article. For this article, the number of grants is more limited, but it still requires some combing through all possible grant opportunities to find the most relevant ones for the largest number of people.

As for the team, it's exciting to see us take the next step and actually activate an ad campaign. There are a few different strategies, so it will be interesting to see the results tomorrow.

Day 15: Friday

⧗ Sue, Executive Office Manager

At Week's End: We kicked off the morning meeting with more homepage upgrades and lots of great suggestions from the team. It would have been nice to start a Friday without a website crash, but these things happen from time to time. We're actively working each week to find a lasting solution.

Not much else to report today, as I'm working a half day. Still, I'll stay focused until noon, tackling daily tasks and doing everything I can to keep our subscribers happy, because without them, there is no us!

🎯 Aaron, Strategic Consultant

Data shows a continuing increase in our social media following, a great sign of our successful campaign. Friday started with an analytics meeting, where we again addressed a site crash that negatively impacted engagement from our emails. Libby and Sue worked on fixing the site as the team continued giving input on potential improvements.

We are really starting to have a modern, well-developed site across the board. Great job by the devs and the entire team.

Nikita is back, which is awesome. Her presence in the meeting was missed, as she has valuable input and expertise in social media and site development.

I finished deploying our Facebook ad campaign, which, at Libby's request, included a video ad and a repeated ad set for conversions instead of site visits. Both are valuable, and running both simultaneously will give us a clear understanding of a successful campaign in the future.

Overall, the entire team did a spectacular job across the board on the site improvements and social media development. Giving GrantWatch the fresh new look it deserves, and we can all be proud of. We're not done yet, but we're almost there!

📊 Nikita, Data Analyst / Media Manager

With Sue out for most of the day, I found myself juggling between helping Chris move forward with the new Foundation pages and tackling the inbox. It's a bit of a balancing act, but I'm pushing to get everything wrapped up before the weekend. Monday's going to be a busy one, and I want to be ready to hit the ground running without anything lingering from this week.

📕 Chris, Web Developer

Building the Heart of the Engine: Libby and I spent the entire day on Zoom working on the grant search page. This page is one of the most important parts of the site; it's the heartbeat of the search engine. We carefully designed it to match the GrantWatch look and feel, ensuring it blends seamlessly when users arrive from the homepage. After a few hours of back-and-forth, we landed on a layout that felt just right. Seeing Libby happy with what we achieved made the effort so worth it. It was a Friday, and I ended the week feeling proud and energized by everything we accomplished.

💡 Pamela, Customer Support Specialist

Aaron reviewed our Instagram statistics, and they show a significant improvement.

Nice to see the growth on Instagram. Glad to see the new page converting. And I like learning about the ad process and tweaking it. It will be exciting to see once everything fully comes together.

🎧 Danika, Grant Support Specialist

Finding Balance: Nikita returned today, and it was great to see how effectively she worked with the development team. We're getting close to a design that will work for all types of users.

Changes were made today in response to AI recommendations. While AI is a helpful tool, there's more to our brand than AI can detect from a simple query. It's important to remember that we are a very niche service. We offer a professional product; however, we also operate in the financial industry, and we must avoid appearing unpolished or unprofessional. To my knowledge, we have not yet asked AI to offer insight to subscription-based models.

I'm feeling hopeful about the direction we're heading and looking forward to regrouping as a team on Monday.

✍️ Lori, Editor and Media Manager

Lots of learning today, and plenty to be excited about! I encountered a few posting hiccups, especially with cross-posting on LinkedIn and TikTok, but I made progress in figuring them out. I also realized the need for a streamlined system to track posts and access creative assets more efficiently. I'm planning to schedule a one-on-one with Aaron to explore whether Metricool has a centralized dashboard feature for this.

Despite the challenges, I got a *ton* accomplished! I scheduled and published all content for Episode 45 using Metricool's smart features. I love the automatic tagging and how easy it is to manage cross-platform content. The chat function made it easy to respond to comments and clear out old replies going back to April. It's incredibly satisfying to see everything coming together.

Content Published Today:

GW Article – FB, LinkedIn, Pinterest, Instagram, X

GWT Ad – FB, LinkedIn, Pinterest, Instagram, X

Libby Ad Reel – FB, LinkedIn, Pinterest, X, Instagram, TikTok

GT Episode 45 – FB, LinkedIn, Pinterest, Instagram, X

Loving the momentum and excited to fine-tune everything next week!

🎨 Adrian, Graphic Artist

Another Friday has been reached, and another carload of work is waiting for me. Let's do this. The day itself was fairly consistent in its scheduling. Work on this and work on that. Someone may notify me of an image they need or any help with that sort of thing. The air conditioner went off, making the already hot day feel hotter. It does score the day as something different from the others. I tend to forget what the individual days of the week are like when Friday arrives. The transient feeling these days makes the week feel like it's up and gone in a blink. Don't really have much to appreciate them. It felt like yesterday that this whole formal strategy of growth and reach started. If it wasn't for this log, I'd forgotten when it started. I make sure the reservoir of images I created doesn't run dry, catching up with me and all. I check the well and make sure I don't work on the edge of deadlines. Hard to keep up sometimes when new work finds its way to sneak up on you. That's just the nature of it all, I suppose. It all passes fast when you get older. Before I know it, my hair will be white, and I'll get some of those spots on my arms.

When I next look in the mirror and see an old man looking back, what face will he have on him? Contentment? Weariness? I can't pretend to predict what I will be like in the future; I doubt I'll care much. As long as I spend time caring about the present, I should be fine. As long as I can remember the present, or past, I guess. It's all memories; we never stop heading to the future. On an unrelated note, Photoshop is working normally again. Splendid.

🎥 Andre, Videographer

The morning began with a sense of purpose, finalizing reels that had lingered in the timeline like stories waiting to be sealed. Once complete, I moved to ads, carving new narratives from raw footage. There were no revelations, no dramatic shifts. Just steady, focused work. A craftsman in his lane.

The week ended with a familiar task: thumbnails. Simple in theory but layered in nuance. Capturing the right moment -the one she envisions is a unique challenge, bordering on impossible without being her. It's not just about finding a smile, but the smile that aligns with how she sees herself.

This became a concern late in the day, so I'll revisit it on Monday. I understand how important the presentation is and remain committed to refining the work until it lands. For now, I'm reviewing frames, searching for that elusive expression: one that feels natural, confident, and unmistakably her.

✉ David, Email Marketing Consultant

Today we had our Zoom meeting, started on time, and made some tweaks to the webpage. I could intervene as the theme was within my understanding. After the meeting ended, we continued discussing changes. This was very nice as the energy was contagious. At first, I felt all the changes were done; however, as things keep getting better, I'm very optimistic that the new design will hit the mark.

🧠 Jeff, Writer

-Now to see Some Campaign Results: So the latest article is in the books. Even though it was a bit hectic, it's good to have the article prepared and submitted for editing. The Ad Campaign results were very encouraging. It looks like our upgrade is yielding some great results!

Day 16: Monday

♟ Sue, Executive Office Manager

A Brand-New Week: We started today by reviewing additional social media updates and the homepage. It seemed to be a very productive meeting. Everyone has good ideas and many new options for change.

◎ Aaron, Strategic Consultant

We began today with Libby, the CEO, unveiling the new site improvements and making significant edits to drive conversions to an even higher level. After the team discussion, I began displaying the continuing growth in social media, which is beating expectations! Per Libby's request, I reduced test ad spend and updated our campaign. Nikita, Lori, and the entire team continue to do an excellent job implementing the new, successful social media strategy. Again, it takes time for a successful Facebook ad campaign to take shape, but we are doing our best to expedite the process.

I led a group discussion with Elissa, Nikita, Lori, and Sue on our LinkedIn strategy and the new structure for Libby's personal page. They will prepare the future content calendars for the upcoming year according to plan. We finished the call by resolving the issues Lori was experiencing with the new platform, and we left on a great note!

I finished the day by refining the audience for our Facebook campaign, per Libby's request.

📊 Nikita, Data Analyst / Media Manager

Today was honestly a blur. I spent most of it deep in our support inbox. I responded to nearly 70 emails. Not quite my personal record (which I think is around 110), but still intense.

Sue managed to get through 15 emails today, most of them after hours. It really highlighted how stretched she is lately, managing everyone in the 20-Day Platform Challenge we are involved with and her usual tasks. It's just more proof that we really need to train one more customer support specialist as the company continues to grow.

💻 Chris, Web Developer

A Pop-up with Purpose: We kicked off the new week with a bang. I worked with Libby, Nikita, and Sue to set up a new pop-up system for both the homepage and grant detail pages. This pop-up is a key feature; it helps guide unpaid users to sign up and subscribe. It took some collaboration and fine-tuning, but we made it both useful and non-intrusive. That pop-up was the highlight of the day.

I also wrapped up the "Category" pages and started working on the "My Account" page. The momentum is still strong, and it feels great to start the week with solid progress.

Pamela, Customer Support Specialist

No meeting for me this morning. Wondering what is going on behind the scenes. Hope to see more changes integrated. The customers keep making suggestions like permanently hiding grants they aren't interested in, and being able to see the funder's name and a brief description. I am curious when our next meeting will be. I also look forward to seeing what other changes will be coming.

Danika, Grant Support Specialist

User Experience: Today has been another productive day. There have been some recent changes to the user experience, including additional steps in the search process. While these adjustments are well-intended, I'm not convinced they're hitting the mark.

Because we operate in a niche, common UX solutions don't always translate well for us. We're close to getting where we need to be, but I'm growing a bit concerned about the current direction. I've been speaking with users who are finding the website increasingly difficult to navigate, and their feedback reinforces the importance of user-centric design.

👍 Lori, Editor and Media Manager

Kicked off the week with a round of post-testing! I scheduled everything for noon, since that's when we're seeing the highest engagement across platforms. There's a noticeable lag in how long it takes for posts to appear, anywhere from a few to ten minutes. That might be a great topic to bring up with Aaron. Maybe staggering post times would help?

GW Platform Testing: LinkedIn, Facebook, and Pinterest all took up to 10 minutes to show up.

Instagram: Metricool showed it as published early, but it didn't appear on the platform. I captured a screenshot for reference.

It's possible the post disappeared due to user error. I'll dig into that more tomorrow. I'm enjoying the challenge of fine-tuning this process and learning the quirks of each platform.

🎨 Adrian, Graphic Artist

There's no such thing as "no more to learn". I'm always learning something about my trade, about anything really. Humans were described as being like a river, always rushing but changing its shape to whatever shape the stream is. We are adaptable things. Wherever we work, we people will adapt to the culture and directives, conforming our work to the expectations of the job. It was a day when the work laid out was consistent with the expectations going in. Over the past few days, I've changed how I create content. The conformation to the river and all that. There'll be a day when the content will need a change, too. The thought doesn't bother me; fluctuations are part of the deal, life and work. So, I did my work, applied what I learned, and became all the better. The river split, and that improvement elevated the engagement adjacent to it. Stagnation isn't an option. Who likes the sound of stagnant water? It can become a hazard if stagnation lasts too long. We always need to progress and flow.

🎥 Andre, Videographer

Today was one of those focused editing days where time disappears. I spent most of it in Premiere, cutting together the rest of a 9-ad set. I used Opus to guide my b-roll ideas, but its inferior AI capabilities led me to outsource the b-roll. It leads to a great combination of AI planting seeds of creativity, while I seek the perfect fit. The facial smoothing took longer than expected(it always does), but the final result looked clean, and the Queen of Grants gave it an A+.

✉ David, Email Marketing Consultant

The day was almost the same as before, Zoom meeting, releasing the camera just for a few seconds, suggesting almost behind the curtain small changes, however at mid-morning some of these suggestions turned in to reality as noticed some flaws in our Mailchimp Templates, after notifying Susan had to come to a decision on sending as they were or wait for developer, that I knew he was buried with work on thousand changes on Website.

🧠 Jeff, Writer - It's Really Coming Together

I finished my latest article. We're gravitating towards a more concise, yet (still) informative article format. Whenever I write, I challenge myself to heed the advice of a former colleague who seared into my brain the following writing strategy: When writing, be as precise as possible without losing the meaning or value of what you're writing. The best litmus test - remove as many words as possible. Then re-read the line. If it's clear & still makes sense, just LEAVE OUT those words.

It's great to be part of the effort to redesign the GrantWatch website. Everyone has at least SOMETHING to add to help finish the puzzle!

Day 17: Tuesday

🏆 Sue, Executive Office Manager

More Updates: Today was packed with continued updates and improvements to the website. We focused on the much-requested eye icon, which is finally in progress. Nikita offered great suggestions for enhancing the foundation search page, and Lori provided a helpful breakdown of which social posts should receive comments and which should be left to grow organically. We also had several discussions around the calls to action on the homepage. It's still a work in progress, but each day moves us one step closer to a polished final product.

🎯 Aaron, Strategic Consultant

We began today by continuing the improvements to the site, which is experiencing record sign-ups again. Nikita, Libby, and I discussed ongoing site improvements and how we can sustain our social media success. We discussed difficulties and solutions while I signed off. Analyzing the incredible social media results, the Facebook campaign is beginning to really sell and convert favorably.

I spent the rest of the day outlining clear filming and editing instructions for the team to ensure coherence, engagement, and professionalism across all posts and platforms.

It was a productive day, and I look forward to successfully completing this awesome project.

📊 Nikita, Data Analyst / Media Manager

Today was full-on. Lori and I spent a good chunk of the day planning out the content calendar for the next 90 days - a whole quarter of the year! It felt like a big undertaking, but we tackled it methodically. I divided up the tasks to keep things moving efficiently, especially since I still had other daily responsibilities to juggle.

Later, I worked with Chris and Libby on finalizing the Foundation page. That part was a bit frustrating. I had already completed most of the tasks last week and organized everything in a document, as Libby had advised, but it seemed that work had completely slipped off the radar. I had to bring it up again to avoid duplicating effort. It's disheartening when work gets overlooked like that.

Overall, today felt a bit overwhelming. There's just *so* much to do. After mapping out the content plan with Lori, I realized that most of the content writing will be on the two of us. The rest of the team either doesn't have the time or isn't as efficient with writing. It's going to be a challenge, but at least Lori and I make a good team!

🖥️ Chris, Web Developer

Today, I focused on building the "Foundation Search" page, which allows users to look up foundations and explore their 990 data pulled from the IRS.

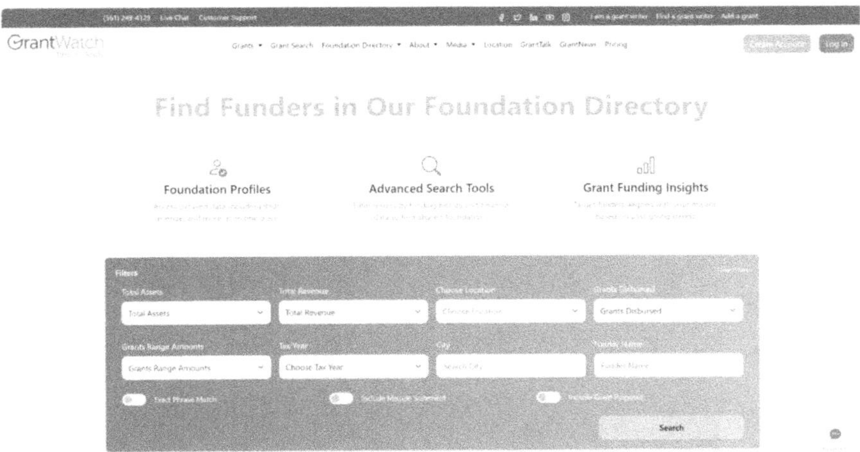

This page is more advanced than most, featuring detailed filters that let users narrow results by the amount given to other foundations, businesses, or individuals. It's a powerful tool for anyone looking to understand how and where funding is distributed. I also set up the links that take users directly to a detailed view with the full 990 breakdown. It felt rewarding to bring more transparency and depth to the platform through this feature. One more important page is taking shape!

💡 Pamela, Customer Support Specialist

Not involved in the meeting today. I see some changes on the homepage. I hcpe we can meet tomorrow and make some tweaks. I think it will be better with fewer steps.

⚫ Danika, Grant Support Specialist

Guiding the User: Today, I spent time working on my multi-user follow-ups and submitted two new articles for Lori to edit, along with my normal tasking.

Aaron shared an analogy that resonated with me, comparing our role to Yoda's, not the hero's. It was a helpful reminder of the role we play in supporting and empowering our users. In other words, the user is the hero of their own grant-seeking journey, and our job is to guide and support them as a mentor would. This perspective reinforces what I've often said: we need to be a helping hand to our users.

✍ Lori, Editor and Media Manager

A super productive day! I worked closely with Nikita on building out the Content Strategy calendar. We created a flexible but structured posting schedule that supports consistency while allowing for creativity and real-time updates. I also mirrored that calendar in my personal Asana board for smoother daily planning.

🎨 Adrian, Graphic Artist

Sometimes technology just doesn't want to collaborate well with me. I've always had some trouble with programs having sort of errors; technology isn't perfect, and that's just the nature of it. It always was that way, since I first held any sort of machine in my hand. Could be a hardware malfunction or a software bug; it'll happen, more so with age and constant use. Learn to take proper care and perform regular maintenance, or you may be in trouble. Some issues that happened today reminded me of that fact. It reminded me of a lot of things. Computational entropy that may have been from planned obsolescence to encourage spending. The ephemeral nature of technology reminded me of time's passage once more. When it's no longer worth repairing, we'll just let it sit somewhere dark till we forget about it. Perhaps that battery has a little bit of juice left in it; many don't see the worth in checking and let it roll under the couch. I keep a lot of old tech stored away, I'll admit, perhaps because I believe there's a chance it'll be of use someday. But I know it'll stay forgotten forevermore. Till writing about it now. I worked on the newsletter, too. That is usually a fairly consistent process, and I'm thankful for that.

🎥 Andre, Videographer

Too many tweaks came from Aaron and Libby across multiple projects, but I powered through. Focusing on integrating feedback into the ads without breaking the flow. Reworked some motion graphics in Adobe After Effects, subtle text punches, not too flashy. The kind of stuff most people don't notice but makes all the difference. Fixed a few awkward OpusClip transitions. Glad I always double-check my videos before exporting.

✉ David, Email Marketing Consultant

Today, we had no Zoom meeting, at least not for me, as there are several different tasks going on, and we have to keep on doing our daily work. I did start sending our Newsletter and other different mail distributions, asking myself how our Newsletter is viewed on the other side of the fence. Interaction with other team members was low; I think they are also catching up on their work.

🧠 Jeff, Writer - The Proof is in the Pudding

I really like that you can enter the first letter of the category & it skips to that alpha section of the (60-category) list!

Also, search results are much more accurate. It ONLY gave me what I wanted, not grants that came close but weren't (otherwise) applicable. Day 18: Wednesday

🏆 Sue, Executive Office Manager

 Out Sick Today: Unfortunately, I wasn't feeling well today, but I still managed to stay up to date on the progress. The team discussed whether Aaron's updates to our social media have increased call and chat volume. They've noticed a slight uptick in calls and more activity in the chat since re-adding the chat feature to the homepage. Pushpendra also added the much-needed GrantWatch logo to key forms, including the check request and Multi-User quote pages, which we've been waiting for. Nikita shared additional helpful input on the archive and foundation pages, and her suggestions continue to be well-received.

🎯 Aaron, Strategic Consultant

The staff felt overwhelmed and unclear about the division of responsibilities on the social media front. So, we started the morning by specifying all responsibilities. We saw strong results and engagement on our posts, so we assigned a team member to handle replies. Brand identity is important; it is represented through a brand's social media presence. It's crucial for us to have a dedicated social media member, first because it will enhance our brand identity and second because we don't want to miss out on potential customers. Using our social media allows us to advertise for free and engage our clientele organically. Not done right, we could be losing out on an incredible amount of potential revenue. We started Google Ads and analytics (not finished yet).

Nikita, Data Analyst / Media Manager

Sue's out sick today, so most of my time has been spent managing the support inbox. It's been a high-volume day - I've responded to 60 messages so far, each one carefully written to address the customer's specific concerns. It's satisfying to make steady progress, but it's definitely a lot to juggle.

In the background, Chris has been continuing work on the site - updating and developing the new pages, so I'm keeping an eye on that as well. It's been a full day, and I'm hoping Sue is well enough to return tomorrow. Honestly, I'm a bit worried about what we'll do if Sue ends up being out longer.

📖 Chris, Web Developer

Spotlight on the Recipients: Today, I worked on the Recipients page, which now highlights the individuals, businesses, and organizations that received funding from various foundations. It's a key part of completing the funding picture, showing not just who's giving, but who's benefiting. The page pulls in real data and makes it easy to explore who received what and from whom. It's starting to feel like every page is connecting into a bigger story, and this one adds real value for users who want to follow the funding trail. Another solid step forward!

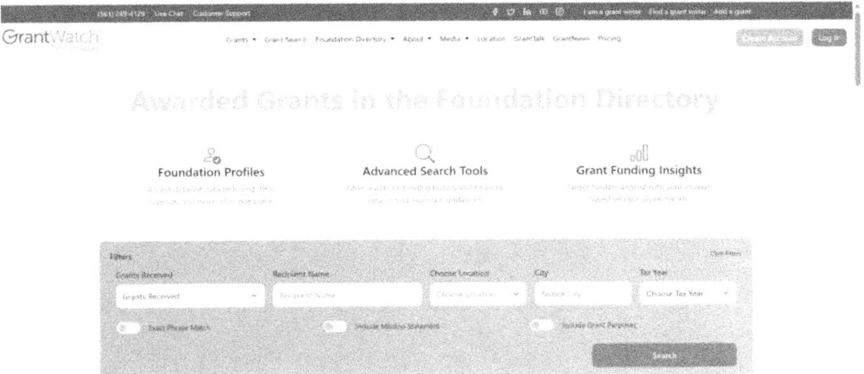

💡 Pamela, Customer Support Specialist

Hopefully, some of my suggestions will be integrated. I think we need to simplify the search further and make it easier to find.

◒ Danika, Grant Support Specialist - Refinements

Today, we continued refining the website, and I'm hopeful that users will appreciate the adjustments we've made.

I also received a few inquiries that appear to have come from our Facebook ads. While they were from individuals, it was encouraging to see engagement. The outreach is working!

✍ Lori, Editor and Media Manager

I spent a large amount of time working with Nikita on the Content Strategy calendar. I also transferred that calendar to my personal posting calendar in Asana. We worked to create a semi-liquid schedule that allows for organic changes but provides a well-executed skeleton to flesh out.

I also spent considerable time working on the "Responsibilities" page of the Content Strategy doc, outlining every task I have on a daily and weekly basis related to content creation. I should point out that the phrase "content creation" doesn't translate well across fields of study and has a different meaning at GW and on social media. Gotta remember that.

🎨 Adrian, Graphic Artist

A standard day of doing the tasks that I needed to accomplish. Everyone is very busy with their tasks as well. We are reaching the end of this revamp. I noticed the website is still in the design process. Hope that all gets figured out. It seems like a lot of work to change it all on the spot, and pretty stressful if I do say so myself. I do like the process of a full assessment of what needs to be changed, and compiling all that information into one form to be referred to afterwards, and making the changes all at once. More easy to work with. Makes the process go more smoothly.

🎥 Andre, Videographer

I had a lot of Photoshop and Premiere work today – mainly cleaning up and finalizing. It felt good to work on the podcast again; there's something satisfying about cutting the clips to the right start, and the masking moves in perfect harmony with the host's movements.

✉ David, Email Marketing Consultant

As work and meetings were done, almost around the clock, and some tasks were reaffirmed, we soon noticed the absence of our office manager, Susan L. She is a very mild and quiet woman, but she is like an onion, present in all dishes, the main ingredient in the kitchen. I do really hope she gets back soon.

🧠 Jeff, Writer

Smoothing Out a Few Rough Edges: Getting closer and closer to achieving the optimal effect on our website home page.

Day 19: Thursday

⏳ Sue, Executive Office Manager

Back At It: Today, we continued refining the homepage, adding and removing elements based on staff suggestions until everything looked and functioned as intended. The team compared the desktop and mobile versions to ensure consistency and smooth functionality. The eye icon is still presenting some issues, but hopefully Chris will be able to tackle that today.

🎯 Aaron, Strategic Consultant

Today's meeting comes on the heels of last night's tragedy in DC. I gave the team a recap of my experience. We continued our discussion about our social media strategy and how to sustain that success once I complete my consulting. (I will miss working with this wonderful team!) I guided Lori through leading today's brief on social media, so that it will continue.

Libby and I continued creating our Google Ads and refining a complete product. We incorporated headlines, keywords, and graphics prepared by Andre, based on my strategy, to match the searcher to the graphic, along with detailed research.

Following the Google ad production, Libby, Lori, Andre, and I analyzed our YouTube performance, and I led the team to understand how professional podcasts produce their videos. So we can emulate a similar strategy to produce quality results. So too on Pinterest: I explained the platform's purpose, how we can and can't produce results, and when we should or shouldn't tailor results for it. Lori was in agreement.

We ended today by detailing site edits and improvements with Chris! We reorganized the header and hero sections to improve the user experience and provide more clarity on the direction off the bat, incorporating the team's suggestions while optimizing for conversion.

Overall, today was really productive, and we have completed all the tasks intended over the past 20 days. All that's left is to launch the final set of Facebook ads based on the dates from our dozens of test results! The team led by Libby continues to show incredible dedication, perseverance, teamwork, and professionalism, going above and beyond to deliver such outstanding results in such a short time!

🔖 Nikita, Data Analyst / Media Manager

Today, Thursday, was one of those days when I felt like I was everywhere at once, wearing multiple hats. I started off in the customer support inbox, responding to messages and making sure nothing was left hanging. From there, I switched gears and worked on updating the Excel sheet with new grants for Israel - steady progress on that front.

Later, I collaborated with Libby and Chris to draft fresh copy for the Foundation Search page. I also spent some time troubleshooting the hide-a-grant icon button with Push, which is still a work in progress, but we're narrowing down the issue.

The highlight of the day was getting a first look at the new homepage that's in development... very exciting to see where things are headed. Before wrapping up, I put together a detailed task list for Chris so he can hit the ground running tomorrow.

All in all, it was a busy but productive day.

💻 Chris, Web Developer - The Final Stretch Begins

Today marked the second-to-last day of the project, and the energy shifted as we began to focus on wrapping everything up. The goal was clear: to finish redesigning every remaining page with the new Bootstrap 5 layout. While the rest of the team began reviewing and improving the main pages we had already completed, I stayed focused on pushing through the remaining redesign work.

Since I had taken on most of the frontend development, I felt the pressure building. With tomorrow being the final day, the weight of the deadline felt more real than ever. It was a bit overwhelming but also motivating. I wanted to finish strong and deliver a polished, complete frontend. The countdown was on, and I was determined to get it done.

💡 Pamela, Customer Support Specialist

It will be sad to see Aaron go. We have made a lot of progress. And I am sure more will continue. I think the home page looks better, less crowded, and more modern. I do think the top could still use less blank space.

☕ Danika, Grant Support Specialist

Meaningful Progress: Today began with a difficult discussion about the heartbreaking and tragic loss of two innocent lives due to the actions of a person consumed by hate and ignorance. I'm grateful that our team created space for us to support each other not just professionally, but as people.

As the day progressed, we refocused on our work and made meaningful changes to the homepage. I felt truly heard during our refinement discussions, which was very encouraging. Push and Chris both completed important tasks vital to our momentum today. I am thankful for their hard work.

👍 Lori, Editor and Media Manager

I was able to test Instagram, and it seems the issues I had yesterday were due to user errors. I have no issues with Metricool that need to be addressed; it works very well. Gauging the processing time: Facebook, LinkedIn, and Pinterest all take between 3 and 7 minutes to complete and appear on the platforms. Instagram is a little longer at about 10 minutes. I have not gauged the process time for reels, but they typically take a while to load, whether using Metricool or posting directly.

I spent a good chunk of my day testing, but also wrote 2 articles, edited 3, worked on the Content Strategy document, coordinated with Adrian on images, and finished my paperwork for the day.

🎨 Adrian, Graphic Artist

Logos happened again. A coworker is in a stressful situation, and I honestly feel for him. I hope today goes well for him. He's a hard worker. I don't interact with him much, but when I do, it's amicable and straightforward. It was a day filled with a bit more meetings. I was assigned the task of assisting with creating Google Ads, finding pictures that matched the prompts shared with me in a document, and working with them. It was later in the day that I was assigned to it, so I'd have to truncate the process and work through the rest of the day, since it's time-consuming. It needed to be finished by tomorrow, the last day of the 20 days. It was interesting. I wonder how the last day will go.

🎥 Andre, Videographer

More hands-on with masking today. It was less about edits and more about precision–matching movements frame by frame. It was a day focused on patience.

✉ David, Email Marketing Consultant

On our Zoom meeting, our CEO requested us to fill a small table containing our daily and weekly content creation task's, at first I thought I would not be included as I handle part of the external mail process, it was a normal and traditional request as on other times in the past years, however, filling just a few lines, it felt strange how a full week could be so minimal on paper, when time is so short to fill the gaps.

🧠 Jeff, Writer

The End is in Sight: It's been an interesting few weeks. I think we've done a great jcb reworking our website and our approach to make our marketing more strategic and effective.

Day 20: Friday

⚗ Sue, Executive Office Manager

Final Meet with Aaron: Today, we focused primarily on reviewing social media insights with Aaron, which was very interesting and helped us understand how users click, engage with, and view our content.

We encountered some PayPal issues and are actively working to resolve them. Nikita, Libby, and Chris continue to work diligently to finalize the website updates.

While today marked our final meeting with Aaron, we're grateful for his wonderful contributions and will carry forward the progress he helped set in motion.

🎯 Aaron, Strategic Consultant

My final day at GrantWatch began with a team meeting to resolve an issue with the payment software involving the entire team. Sue was on and active despite feeling terribly under the weather; her dedication to GrantWatch is commendable.

I walked the team through the Facebook ads we've completed and analyzed the top-performing ads, creating a final campaign for Facebook.

As I wrap up my time with GrantWatch, I look back at what we've accomplished in just one short month of consulting. A total site revamp and modernization, a successful and booming social media strategy, organizational structure, a money-making Facebook Ad Campaign, and, most importantly, wonderful business relationships with the entire team at GrantWatch.

My time at GrantWatch was enjoyable and informative. I truly appreciate this great team welcoming me and allowing me to share my knowledge with them to benefit the company. There were challenges, differences of opinion, and a wide variety of changes, but I am proud of the results we produced together.

I deeply value my relationship with Ms. Hikind and the incredible GrantWatch team. Working with them was a great privilege, and I am thrilled to see the growth and excited about what's to come. I wish the team and GrantWatch all the best in the future!

Nikita, Data Analyst / Media Manager

Today marked the final major push in our website makeover journey. Reflecting on how far we've come - from those chaotic first steps to where we are now - it's truly been a roller coaster.

I managed to write four new articles for GrantNews, helping us get ahead on content. Chris and I also coordinated to ensure all our sites were properly indexed, and I spent time managing the support inbox and handling a range of other tasks that came up throughout the day.

It's been a demanding process, with its fair share of highs and lows. Honestly, I'm relieved that we're nearing the finish line. I've been operating at full capacity, and I'm looking forward to finally shifting my focus back to other critical tasks that have been on hold.

Chris, Web Developer – A Strong Finish

Today was the final day of the project, and I'm proud to say, I finished strong. I wrapped up all the remaining pages, bringing every piece of the new design together. It was a very rewarding feeling to look back and see how far the site had come. The redesign not only gave GrantWatch a modern, polished look but also made the platform easier to use and more inviting for new members.

Finishing everything on time felt like a huge win. After weeks of focused work, collaboration, and fine-tuning, we now have a site that's visually aligned with our mission and ready to grow with our audience. I'm excited for what's ahead and proud of what we built.

💡 Pamela, Customer Support Specialist

Aaron's last day. We will all miss him. He helped make so many changes in such a short period of time. Glad to see we have some high-converting ads. We really all pulled together as a team. And will be interesting to see how we grow with all of these changes. It was exciting to see how much work we all accomplished in such a short time. I'm looking forward to the changes and modernization of GrantWatch, which will help us help more customers.

⚫ Danika, Grant Support Specialist

Strategy & Teamwork: Over the past 20 days, our team has proven we can collaborate effectively. This deep dive has established a foundation for building momentum that will ultimately support long-term impact and a more intuitive, welcoming platform. I am proud to have played a part in improving our customers' user experience. I look forward to the perpetual benefits of this collaboration.

✍ Lori, Editor and Media Manager

Today started with a meeting with the whole staff, and Aaron, Adrian, Andre, and I had a productive discussion about the reels, podcast, etc.

Aaron gave info on Pinterest. It wasn't really anything I didn't already know. Pinterest is best visited by women who are one of the following: Moms, wives, crafters, media artists, graphic artists, photogs, designers, and the list goes on. It was, however, very helpful to get corroboration on the information I already possess.

Every post that pertains to the Pinterest crowd is super colorful, crafty-looking, artsy, and the like. My reasoning is that Pinterest doesn't attract the grant crowd, so we don't see much movement on that platform, but you never know who's off work and scrolling away.

I was asked to present analytics information on the spot. Using Metricool, I came off sounding very informed. This will be my task in the future to share with Libby and the entire staff.

The scheduling and posting today went off without a hitch. I was very pleased with my ability to use the platform to some degree of success.

Thank you to Aaron for showing us the ropes of Metricool and helping with the construction of the new website. The coming months will be a test to see whether the changes to posting and the use of Metricool are worth it, and I'm really looking forward to it! The new website is up and running, working well with some fine-tuning here and there, and the whole experience has been well worth the effort.

🎨 Adrian, Graphic Artist

The last entry of these journals. I had a lot of thoughts and shared most of them. Regardless, today played out the same as the other days, a lot of work and a lot of meetings. It was described as crunch time; everyone was all hands-on deck. I figured it was. I am familiar with the term by now. I am sure the others are as well. The images were brought up again, and needed to be made into square and vertical formats as well. Fine then, I'll do so and get them done.

Went to a meeting with three others, collaborated on what to write on the images, and that was another thing done for the day. Check that off and move on to the next project. The website is still being worked on, from the sounds of it. A change here and a change there from what I saw. I hope they find what they need when editing the website. Looks and sounds like a lot of work. A lot of things here sound like a lot of work, but making the website looks the most intensive. The sky looks pretty overcast out here where I work, if I had to switch gears a bit. Has been for a bit, guess the sky over here likes its cover. I like it too; there is a clearness in the color it gives to the world. A clarity of everything. So much grey. It's nice. Helps in my concentration. Couldn't help looking out the window and reminiscing a bit.

🎥 Andre, Videographer

Wrapped up all paid formats today: vertical, square, widescreen. I also continued editing the latest GrantTalk episode.

Hoping the team finds more structure and momentum soon. With a shift from scattered to intentional. Sometimes there are too many hands in things. I hope the team stays structured with our Asana content calendar.

May structure, growth, and order rise in all of us.

✉ David, Email Marketing Consultant

Last day on this series, just got used to doing this, a bit nostalgic already. Today we had our Zoom meeting, just a bit later than usual, guess that so many things to do, contributed to get the rest of us a bit later, soon the meeting went to high density metrics on Facebook and from the beginning to the end I really could not catch many words, maybe because I was sending mails like crazy and uploading state audiences to clear my board or maybe just because it was really hard to hear as Aaron speaks a bit fast. As happens many times, just kept following the conversation on Teams.

🧠 Jeff, Writer

It's a Wrap! So, we've come to the end of our 20-Day Platform Challenge journal. I think it's been a good learning experience. Hopefully, the lessons learned can be translated into better efficiency and productivity by everyone.

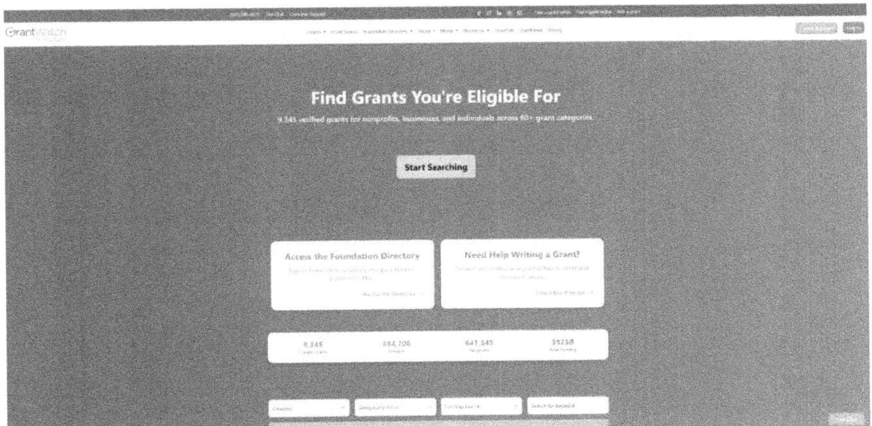

Getting out of the Weeds

Aaron said goodbye; he enjoyed his time with us, but, as he told me from the beginning, he did not want a full-time job. We do stay in contact and help each other. I bounce ideas off of him, and he does the same to me. We keep each other sharp.

We are better for having worked with him, but now it is time to hire someone and hand over the day-to-day operations. I started interviewing in June 2025. It was not easy to interview, check references, and conduct references for a senior-level position.

We started and stopped with people a few times. Hopefully, I have finally found my person in Ariel.

I want to share with you what I quoted to Ariel and will leave it here for him to review as well. I read this in a 2025 *Travel Weekly* interview with Richard Fain. He recounted the four pillars of the strategic plan he presented to his board in 1988, when he took over as CEO of Royal Caribbean Group. 1. Don't screw it up. 2. Improve revenue. 3. Reduce costs. 4. Moderate growth.

Simple! It says all that I want to impart to my new Team Lead.

After reading it, I was looking forward to my Monday morning conversation with my new hire. For me, GrantWatch is not about piling on features no one asked for or charging for fluff that doesn't serve the mission. It's about giving people exactly what they need, nothing more.

That focus shapes everything we're building on GrantWatch now. If you have read my first book, *The Queen of Grants from Teacher to Grant Writer to CEO*, I included black-and-white images showing GrantWatch's growth, and we are still growing now with Ariel, changing and evolving with the times and technology. Today's website, in February 2026, is an improved version of what it was when Aaron left in May 2025.

My goal is to reduce the time grant seekers spend searching for opportunities, cut down the hours my team spends creating detailed grant pages, and eliminate the blank-page panic that comes with writing proposals. I want to give every grant seeker a smart, supportive companion that helps them find, write, and win faster and with confidence. I also want to help them stay organized and have a trusted space for their organization.

Getting out of the weeds, for me, means no longer having to personally supervise every staff member. I have done that for the last 16 years. That's the job of my new number one person: to build organization, structure, and responsibility as we continue to grow. It means I am no longer spending my days untangling or micromanaging tasks.

I look forward to having more time to guide the company into the future while also having time to write children's books, young adult novels, new novels, business and organization tools, and *The Queen of Grants 3:* all of which you can find on *libbyhikind.com.*

New hires often want to rebuild everything their way. They do not have the history I have. So hopefully I will be around for a long time.

Here is an example of why history matters: I did not want to be the boss who says no to everything – that would not be a way to keep an employee. We looked at my Google Ads account, which was performing fine. My new Team Lead pushed for a specific campaign type. I had already tried it before. I let him run it for a short time. The results were the same as what I had previously experienced, so we removed it.

That moment reminded me why history matters; not everything needs reinventing, sometimes it is just refining. And we found his strength on Facebook to get us to 3x ROI, to not accept everything the Google advisor says, to organize our devs and Asana tickets, and, most recently, to organize content and socials. He keeps the waters calm.

Here are my pillars for my staff: Don't screw it up. Protect what works. Know our history. Listen and develop what our subscribers want. Keep the wins intact and build upon those. Improve revenue. Optimize the proven. Test with intent. Scale what earns.

I want to semi-retire and feel confident that I will stay relevant, continue reading and discovering new innovations, exploring what's next, and then trusting my number one to run with those ideas, or better yet, to bring new ones to me.

That's where this next chapter begins, using technology, especially AI, to do what humans can't do alone: to work smarter, faster, and more creatively. Let me introduce you to our new AI Grant Writing Tool, AI Grant Finder, AI Foundation, and Recipient Directory, and our wonderful new and improved Grants calendar. Our tools are your assistant, not your grant writer. They do not replace your passion and your backstory.

IV: AI in Grant Writing

Before we go any further, I want to be clear that what I am going to explain goes far beyond GrantWatch.

Every organization eventually reaches a point where the idea of working harder stops working for the company. At some point, the system itself becomes the problem.

That is the moment when leaders have a choice. You can keep asking people to carry more, stretch the day longer, hire more people, or you can redesign the work so people can do it better.

That is the choice we faced.

What We Learned About the Needs of Our Own Team

When we watched our own team at work, we leaned into a question we had been circling for years: How can we reduce pressure on our team to boost productivity and focus on work that requires judgment, experience, and care?

What you are about to read is not a story about technology for technology's sake. It is about responsibility. It is about protecting human judgment, reducing frustration, and building systems that support, not drain, the people doing it.

Whether you run a nonprofit, small business, municipality, or tribal program, the same question applies. Where is your team spending time that does not truly require them, and what becomes possible when you give them that time back?

That question changed everything for us. This chapter is about that answer. It is not about replacing grant researchers and grant writers. It is not about automating decisions.

It is about using the new tools available, like AI, where they belong. It is about how, for us, the answer was to use AI behind the scenes to support research and reduce frustration. And for our subscribers, to provide them with the public-facing, faster, and better tools to find the grants they need to fund their causes.

Let me take you into my confidence and tell you what we built and why we made those decisions. I want to share with you how you can use the new tools to successfully find and apply for grants in your own work.

Working Smarter After the Challenge Ended

By the time we finished the 20-Day Platform Challenge, one thing was clear. We were not done. Those twenty days were intense. Our staff pushed hard, worked together, tested ideas, fixed problems, and refreshed the platform in real time. And yes, some of my staff waxed poetic.

But something more important happened; what started as a challenge became proof of something bigger. We could move faster without cutting corners. We could collaborate better when everyone understood the goal. And most importantly, we could see where our time was being stretched too thin. The challenge showed us what was possible. Now let me tell you what it means for you.

What We Want the Reader to Take with Them

If there is one thing I hope you carry forward, it is this: although there are no shortcuts in grant funding, there are always better systems. AI is not a replacement for thinking, planning, or passion. Used well, it simply gives you back time so you can focus on the parts of the work that only you can do.

Whether you are searching for grants, managing a team, or building something new, the question is the same: are your systems working for you, or are you working for your systems? Once you start asking that question honestly, real progress becomes possible.

The 20-Day Platform Challenge opened the door for what was possible and removed the fear of new technology. They started asking what AI could do to streamline their work.

Keep in mind that I originally wanted to start with the back-end, but I could not convince my research staff that AI would help them. Now they are onboard.

The five tools we were developing showed our grant researchers more of what was possible for their tasks. If we could do what we did for the public, what could we do for the behind-the-scenes grant researchers, grant associates, and our editors and publishers of the grants on our website?

Our team was spending hours on tasks that were necessary but repetitive: sorting, organizing, cross-checking, and preparing information that still needed human review before it ever reached a subscriber. No one was wasting time, but the system itself demanded too much of it.

Why Existing Tools Were Not Enough

Why were the off-the-shelf AI or other tools not a good fit for GrantWatch's specific needs? Basically, the same answer I gave my developers in 2010 when we were building the original GrantWatch, and they offered me prepackaged templates. I told them then, and

I told them now, "I am not going to conform the needs of my subscribers to the technology, I am going to configure technology to the needs of my subscribers."

I want to take you back to about six months before the 20-Day Platform Challenge. I was ready to start using AI and bought a piece of hardware for $20K to send to our hosting provider, so they could provide us with enough juice (computing power) to run AI.

The part was coming from overseas, and I do not want to malign the manufacturer, but they sure sent us a lemon. And then when they replaced it, the hosting provider did not have the cooling station power to run it. All is well that ends well. We did not move into the tech world, and everything got returned except the cost of postage.

Over the course of the 20-Day Platform Challenge, we learned that we could purchase AI subscription tokens, buy AI time, and let the AI provider control the hardware.

Hire Tech People to Propel Your Company

After the 20-Day Platform Challenge, I also learned that I needed to hire a full-time person who loved technology and was already familiar with the latest software programs. It took us from May to

September, and a few tries of people in between, to find Ariel, the new Marketing & Tech Team Lead for GrantWatch.

He then quickly got us looking for an AI web developer to help us with the behind-the-scenes AI initiatives to streamline our systems. That developer works directly with the team that posts the grants, spends 8 hours a day with the research team leads, and feels their pain.

Until September 2025, I had spent every day, 6 days a week, in development for both front-end and back-end. I was permanently tethered to my desk from 9 AM to 2 PM, and sometimes in the middle of the night, just working on development with screen shares with developers, just to keep the momentum. GrantWatch moves like a train that never stops for long. If you pause, you don't just slow down; you miss the next few stops entirely.

Ariel became my relief. I was finally able to work on my business and not directly in it. He placed developers to work with the teams that produce, and he manages all of them.

GrantWatch Uses Humans to Review the Grants

One of our most complex initiatives was integrating AI into our editorial workflows so information from source websites can be mapped directly into structured database fields. This requires handling multiple website layouts, inconsistent formatting, and varied file types, while ensuring that the AI remained 100% faithful to the source content. This significantly reduced editorial workload and publishing time while preserving accuracy through mandatory human review.

We write some of the text for a grant posting, copy text from the funder, and review every field in the grants posted against the funder's website and offerings.

Imagine asking a super-smart robot to help write a grant description. It spits out something that sounds confident and totally believable, except sometimes it's just making stuff up. That's what we call AI hallucinations. The robot confidently invents fake stats, wrong dates, made-up references, or details that don't exist. It happens because these tools are great at sounding right, but they don't really know things the way a person does. They just predict the next word based on patterns they've seen.

I recently had to research some legal stuff and case law to back up what I thought was correct. I got the absolute best lawyer's letter, citing case after case – it was too good to be true. So, I did not believe it as I have been taught that "If it is too good to be true, it probably is not", over and over again. Guess what? Most of the cases were made up – they sounded real but were not!

In the grant world, where every fact, number, and promise matters and real money and real impact are at stake, even a single hallucination can confuse applicants. That's exactly why we don't just let AI or auto-tools push a grant post live without a human giving it a good read-through.

My office was contacted by an individual who had been working as an independent contractor for a competitor with more grants than we had. Our customer support staff occasionally receives comments from subscribers about the poor quality of their grant postings. But we figured, why not give him a chance? Let's see how he works so quickly. He promised to deliver postings at a level faster than our most experienced grant associates. So, we gave him some training, and he kept saying, "I know, I know, I have experience."

On a trial basis, we tested him out, and what we found was that he submitted AI grant descriptions of the source pages we gave him, and the work was hallucinated. We understood from him that what he submits is what is published on the website as is. He said he had a whole team ready to come on board, and I told him and them to stay where they are.

Our editorial team is a team of educated, real people who jump in for that final check. They are looking for anything that sounds too good or too weird to be true. The team double-checks facts, citations, and numbers against what we know, ensuring the wording is clear, fair, and won't trip anyone up.

We verify the data against the primary source material and official guidelines and confirm facts. We look for anything missing in the description and ensure the AI hasn't filled those gaps with fabricated information. We rewrite any robotic, overly polished, or questionable AI-generated language into clear, accurate, warm, and trustworthy English that grant writers and applicants can rely on.

AI Is a Powerful Assistant

It organizes scattered ideas into clean bullet points, suggests stronger phrasing, fixes grammar, and speeds up drafting. But it cannot be trusted to determine truth or completeness on its own. Humans still have accuracy and trust. We review every single grant post so that what reaches the public is honest, complete, and rock-solid. No invented details, no fairy-tale fill-ins, just the real information grant seekers need to succeed.

Our 5 Latest AI-Powered Tools

Let me walk you through our five shiny new AI-powered tools, developed since my first book. We started developing the tools with the 20-Day Platform Challenge. They were built by my team to make your life a whole lot easier when hunting for grants and putting proposals together. My team has my ear; they listen carefully when you call and address your concerns in our meetings.

The newest tools are super straightforward and super helpful: The AI Grant Writing Tool, The AI Grant Finder, The AI Foundation Directory Search Tool, the AI Grant Recipient Search Tool, and the new My Grant Calendar, now downloadable to your personal calendar.

Grant Writing and AI

If you've ever started a grant application, taken the headings, placed them on a blank page, and just sat there, frozen, as if anything you write might mark both you and your organization for life, then you know the pain. It's not that you don't have most of the plan developed in your head; it's getting it down on paper as a cohesive sales pitch.

For years, I've watched nonprofit founders, small business owners, and dreamers with golden missions all freeze when they start writing a grant proposal, at the same place: page one.

Back in 2012, I tried to solve that paralysis by launching *GrantWriterTeam.com*, a platform where organizations could find real grant writers to help bring their visions to life. It worked. They're still using it today, and it's helped thousands of organizations get the help they need.

But here's what I've always said, and still believe: "Write your first grant yourself." If for nothing else, it is when you will gather all the information about yourself and your organization to be a grant contender. And who knows? You may have a talent for grant writing and win the grant.

Why? Because that first grant writing attempt will be stronger than any grant professional could ever write. Going through the process yourself will show you what your ideas sound like when they are written straight from your heart and in your own words.

In my first book, I wrote about my first grant and my win, when only one in four grants were awarded by the Tandy Corporation in the USA that year. And that is where this all began.

And now, coming full circle, I have worked closely with my development and customer success teams to build the GrantWatch AI Grant Writing Tool. It was created not to replace you, but to remind you. "You've got this!" It's your safety net, your starter spark, your guide to breaking through that blank page and finding your voice on the other side.

When you work in a Grok or ChatGPT account, it is advisable to disable the setting used to train the public AI model. With our tool, we do not want you to delete your work, as it is training the model for you, not for anyone else.

How will AI Help or Hurt Your Grant Application?

As I emphasized in a GrantWatch announcement in August 2025, "Passion is the heartbeat of a winning grant proposal. Our AI Grant Writing Tool gives users a powerful starting point to craft drafts, which they can infuse with their mission's passion; all within our affordable MemberPlus+ subscription."

Why Human Passion Must Lead

Having interviewed 59 people on *GrantTalk*, I often asked about grant applications that were noticeably written by AI and what happened to those proposals. Given that these interviews took place from February 2024 through May 2025, as AI was emerging, the responses were mostly the same: it was clear to the reader that AI was used, and they generally did not fund those proposals.

It brings me back to when students would submit store-bought term papers that totally missed the assignment's mark. Having AI write your entire grant application is like turning in one of those term papers from back in the day, the kind that missed the whole point of the assignment. Sure, it looks neat, reads smoothly, even sounds smart in some places, but it's empty where it counts.

AI can polish your words, tighten your sentences, even help you clarify your thoughts, but it can't feel your mission. It doesn't know your community, your passion, or the late nights you've spent crunching the data and shaping the plan. It can rearrange your sentences, but it can't dream your dream.

The ideas, the data, and the strategy must be yours. A grant application isn't just paperwork; it's your story, your case for why your vision deserves to live. If it sounds too good to be true, it probably isn't true. The magic is never in the polish; it's in the purpose, the backstory, the budget, and the plan that is possible within the realm of your organization.

Can you convince the reader that you fully understand the mission of the funder, that your needs match their mission, that you have set the goals and objectives, developed activities and evaluation, all within the budget allocated, and have the organizational capacity to run the program? There are no shortcuts for getting things right! But there are ways to reduce time and work more efficiently. That is the only way to use AI.

Our AI Grant Writing Tool

We all know from the interviews, real-world stories, and plain old experience that AI should never write a full grant for you. Doing that would remove your passion, your unique voice, and the precise alignment of your mission with the funders'. It would disqualify you for not following directions and missing the intent of the funding opportunity.

This was one of the challenges we also faced when developing our AI Grant Writing Tool, and we successfully built an AI model that does not hallucinate.

"This tool (The GrantWatch AI Grant Writing Tool) draws directly from my experiences," as noted from a press release appearing on Yahoo Finance August 2025: "Born from the insights in Hikind's book, *The Queen of Grants: From Teacher to Grant Writer to CEO*, the tool empowers users to create tailored, professional grant proposals without the need for costly consultants. It levels the playing field, just like GrantWatch always has."

Grant applications aren't cookie-cutter; they are personal stories of your impact told in exactly the way the funder asks for them. Hallucinations will creep in when you skip providing the details and let AI guess instead of feeding it your real facts, your real passion, your real data.

That's why our AI Grant Writing Tool was designed differently. It's built to organize your ideas and support you the way real grant writers work: section by section, starting with your own input, giving you a strong foundation for a first draft, and then stepping back so you can infuse it with everything that makes your organization shine.

It flows, step by step, through the most common sections of most grants, using the mapping process I outlined in the last chapter of my first book in The Queen of Grants series, ***The Queen of Grants: From Teacher to Grant Writer to CEO.***

Right now, you are probably wondering about costs, since we are discussing new features on GrantWatch. To use the AI Grant Writing Tool to organize your thoughts, you only need a plain member account without payment. However, to use our AI to revise your writing section by section, in your own voice, you need a paid MemberPlus+ account.

I want to explain to my readers that AI is not free. AI tools come with real, usage-based costs; every search, every revision, every query increases our expenses. Presently, we cover the increased costs ourselves and maintain a flat-rate subscription fee for GrantWatch and all new AI features, hoping that, as technology matures, costs will stabilize or decline.

Why? Because GrantWatch believes in leveling the playing field for all organizations, large and small. Our mission holds true 25 years later as we move forward.

What we see with our AI Grant Writing Tool is that the more it is used by an individual, the more on-target it becomes for that grant writer. As you use it, you are training your own model, and it seems to be getting better with each use. GrantWatch's AI was built to work with the data you input. That is why our tool is better than grant writing with generative AI. Your ideas are limited to your profile and do not cross the gates we have set.

There is a tab on the navigation bar called AI Grant Writing Tool, where you will find it. You will want to create a new proposal draft (name it whatever feels good to you; "New Proposal 3" is simple and works great, or use the grant title to better organize).

In my last book, I showed you how to use AI to create goals and objectives. I cannot stress this enough, and I am sorry to be so blunt, but a grant application fully written by AI is trash, because that is where it will land.

You must have a program or project to write a grant application. You need to know why it is needed and who it benefits, how you will implement it, how you will evaluate it, and what the budget is. AI can assist with sections or paragraphs, but only if you provide the relevant information. And if it is boring, it means it lacks your passion.

If you're writing the proposal for a specific grant on GrantWatch, enter the GrantWatch ID, and it will auto-fill the official title, the funder's direct link, and key details, so you're always locked in on the right opportunity.

Then the magic begins: The tool guides you through every essential section that strong proposals need, such as: organizational history and capacity, staff and financial info, previous grants, legal status, community engagement, the specific needs your project tackles (add real data and stories), project goals, clear measurable objectives, planned activities, evaluation plan, budget breakdown, in-kind contributions, sustainability strategy, dissemination plan, and replicability.

These aren't random sections. They have been drawn from most grants. For each section, you get thoughtful, guided prompts to spark your thinking. You answer in your own words first, pouring in your passion, your facts, your mission. Then hit "Improve with AI". Here is where you need a paid subscription – so you may want to take care of that before you begin. You are going to improve with the AI section by section.

The tool takes what you've given it, and tightens the language, boosts clarity, improves flow, strengthens the narrative, and stays true to what you wrote.

You can go back into it and straighten out anything that is off a bit, and hit refine with AI, or just take it and plug it into your grant application – but read it carefully!

We designed the tool to avoid inventing details and hallucinations, because it works from your input. Save, review, move to the next section, repeat.

If your input is lacking, AI will fill in the blanks, and that may be far off-base, and that is on you for not providing the details.

When you've worked through everything, you can produce a complete first-draft proposal. And here's the most important part: This is only the beginning.

You don't submit the tool's output as-is. You never do. You take that draft, read every word, revise it, mold it, customize it to follow the funder's directions to the exact letter, no compromises. The funder may have a completely different set of prompts or questions, so you need to evaluate which sections you need to respond to. You might want to include the funder's question or prompt in your text of the closest section in our AI Grant Writing Tool to help you refine your work.

Grant writing is subject to space limitations, such as character or word count. Our tool will provide you with a character count that includes spaces. This may help you pare down your writing to the section's character count. You can modify within the sections until you have the right count.

Add more of your passion, tweak for tone, double-check compliance, and weave in any new insights. Each grant is unique, and only you can ensure it flows as the funder requires.

This tool saves you huge chunks of time on first drafts and early revisions, so you can focus on what matters most: infusing every section with your organization's authentic mission, ensuring perfect alignment, and delivering a proposal that's undeniably yours.

The GrantWatch AI Grant Writing Tool is not here to replace you; it's here to lift you up, help you submit stronger applications, and give you the edge in a competitive world.

That's the power we're building together at GrantWatch. Tools that honor the human heart of grant writing while harnessing AI to make the process calmer, faster, and more doable.

You've got passion; now you've got the perfect partner to help it shine brighter. And we want to hear from you. How can we improve it further to suit your needs?

How AI Supports Grant Search Without Replacing Judgment

GrantWatch has always been about leveling the playing field. Individuals, small businesses, nonprofits, Tribal Nations, and municipalities all deserve access to the same quality of information without needing insider language or endless hours of research. AI allows us to carry that mission forward, not by changing who we are, but by working smarter at what we already do well.

Our tools do not replace planning, preparation, or judgment. They simply make the research side of the work less overwhelming. Think of what follows as a set of helpers, not answers.

The GrantWatch AI Grant Finder

I promised you 5 new tools. The AI Grant Writing tool is number one. The AI Grant Finder is number two.

When I first started grant research, it meant going to the Foundation Center in Manhattan and sitting there for hours. You had to learn the system's language just to get results. One wrong term, and you'd miss opportunities you didn't even know existed. I would leave with handwritten notes, go home, and type everything up, hoping I had not overlooked something important.

When Google came along, it felt like a gift. Searching became easier, faster, and more accessible. But it also created a new problem. Too much information and not enough filtering. Grants that were already closed. Grants you would never qualify for. Grants that looked promising until you read the fine print.

GrantWatch was created to solve that exact problem. It was created to clean up the noise of deadlines and dead ends. To rewrite grant-speak into English for the professional who did not grow up in the grant industry.

When we started the website, we focused on categories, verified deadlines, and the information people needed to decide whether a grant was worth their time. That philosophy has never changed.

Our AI Grant Finder tool is a real game changer, built to support your process, not rush it. The tool focuses on what is available right now, the grants that are open and ready for you to pursue. It helps you ask better questions, narrow your focus, and spend your time on grants that align with your mission. Instead of forcing you into rigid categories, the AI allows you to use the natural language of your organization. You can search using the words and phrases that reflect your mission, and the tool follows your thinking rather than placing you in a predefined box.

Now you can type a couple of words that describe what you do. For example, "food" and "California", if you run a food pantry or something similar. Hit the green button and boom. The AI hands you a nice, tight list of grants (148 when I tried it – today there may be more or fewer) that are relevant to food, nutrition, or related work in California. Some mention food straight-up, others are close cousins. You skim the titles and short blurbs, see what feels right, then click in for the full scoop. The AI Grant Finder is perfect for when your mission doesn't fit neatly in the usual categories, or you just want fast, spot-on results.

Now, let me clarify how access works. The advanced grant search remains free to use. The AI Grant Finder is available with a paid subscription. However, we do allow users one free search to become familiar with the tool.

The GrantWatch AI Foundation Directory

The AI Foundation Directory is the third tool.

Once you've searched for open opportunities, note that if we have foundation data, there will be a button for the 990 Report (we regularly add new available IRS data for our subscribers, as it becomes available).

You can also take the next step after searching for current grants: start searching for foundations that have previously supported the same mission you were looking for in current grant opportunities.

Look beyond the present moment and into the donors themselves. Inside the AI Foundation Directory, you can explore the history of giving through 990 filings and see the story funders have already told with their past donations.

Using Public Data and 990s More Intentionally

When you read a funder's 990s, you're not just studying data, you're listening to their values. Their choices reveal what compelled them in the past and what kind of change they are trying to bring to the world.

Donors don't give because an organization is short on resources. They give because they want to transform lives. The funders' passion for their mission drives every decision they make, whether it's a major foundation or a family fund giving quietly year after year. If you read Chapter 1 of this book or watched the complete videos on the *GrantTalk* tab on GrantWatch or on YouTube, you hear that funders are committed to their mission. They want the projects they fund to be the catalyst for accomplishing their vision of making the world a better place, one grant at a time.

While our advanced search filters give you structure, AI gives you freedom. Together, they help you see the heart behind the funding and the impact pattern that matters to each donor. Your networking and grant writing work then becomes the art of showing how your mission carries that same spark forward, how your passion aligns with theirs, and how the transformation they care about is already alive in the work you do.

When using the Foundation Directory, you can search by name, keyword (say "school" or "arts"), location, how much money they have (their assets) to give away, and what categories they have given to in the past, according to tax year. We have charted and graphed a great deal of information from the raw data for you, which you can look into yourself as well. It is all there on our website, from simple analysis to more complex research.

Type "school," hit search, and you'll see a clean list of foundations that care about education. You can keep dialing it in by picking specific terms like elementary, high school, college, preschool, or whatever industry you are in.

The Grants Recipient Search

This is the fourth tool I spoke about. You can get to the Grant Recipient Search by clicking the Foundation Directory tab on the navigation bar. There, you can search for the name of a similar organization (maybe one in the next town over or one that does the same kind of thing as you do). Hit search, and it pulls up recipients.

You can also click the name of an organization that received a grant listed on a funder's page in the Foundation Directory and click each year to see the amount of funding they received and the kinds of projects that captured the funder's vision.

The AI Grant Recipient Search is where the deeper understanding begins. If you want to know who's getting money for work like yours, the grant recipients listed are linked to descriptions of their organizations.

If you locate the grant recipient, you can see exactly who gave them grants, how much, and in which years (a lot of this comes straight from their 990s).

It's a goldmine for spotting local funders you might never have found otherwise, or seeing which big players are supporting organizations just like yours.

These four tools (AI Grant Writing Tool, AI Grant Finder, AI Foundation Search, and AI Grants Recipient Search) are designed to make applying for grants feel less overwhelming and way more doable. They help you find the right opportunities, write better proposals quicker, and discover funding sources you didn't even know existed.

Grant Calendar

The fifth tool is the Grants Calendar. I cannot begin to count how many times this was submitted as a ticket in our management software to enhance the calendar, but we never got it to where I wanted it. Thank you, Ariel. When we discussed everything that I wanted done before I completed *The Queen of Grants 2*, you made it happen.

And just now, as I'm closing my book, technology finally caught up. Or maybe my Team Lead had the solutions we were forever looking for to do this right for you. We revisited our "My Grant Calendar" and enhanced it to deliver a more powerful, user-friendly experience for grant seekers.

We used modern tools and user feedback and transformed it into a true command center for managing your grant pipeline. The grant calendar helps you track deadlines, plan ahead, and stay on top of opportunities so nothing slips through the cracks.

These updates make staying organized feel far more manageable, whether you're juggling multiple applications, tracking reporting requirements, or forecasting upcoming cycles.

Here are the key enhancements to the My Grant Calendar: a one-click integration with personal calendars that lets you easily add grant deadlines to your preferred calendar app (Google Calendar, Apple Calendar, Outlook, Yahoo, and more) with dedicated export buttons. This syncs reminders directly into your daily workflow, complete with native notifications to keep you on track.

A major addition is the true calendar view, providing a visual calendar interface (weekly or monthly) that displays all your saved grants and their key dates at a glance. Spot overlapping deadlines, identify high-pressure periods, and plan your time more effectively.

We also created a detailed table view that lets you switch to a clean, sortable table for an at-a-glance overview of your saved grants. View essential details, including funder name, deadlines, status, and custom note entries. The table view is a quick way to review and encourage team collaboration, or to support in-depth pipeline management.

The quick preview and inline notes let you view any saved grant without leaving the calendar. Add, edit, or review notes on the spot to capture ideas, status updates, next steps, or attachments, streamlining your workflow and keeping everything in one place.

You can also use the advanced status tracking and filtering: *Work in Progress, Ready to Submit, Submitted, Awarded, Denied, and Archived,* and filter the entire calendar by status. Focus instantly on what's urgent, like upcoming submissions or post-award obligations, all while maintaining a clear picture of your overall progress.

These improvements build on what My Grant Calendar has always offered, now supercharged for today's fast-paced grant environment. With daily-updated grants from GrantWatch integrated seamlessly, you can save opportunities in seconds and watch your calendar populate automatically with verified deadlines.

Whether you're a nonprofit chasing impact funding, a small business exploring growth grants, or an individual pursuing personal opportunity, these enhancements reduce administrative stress, boost efficiency, and help you submit stronger applications on time.

I'm glad to end this book with My Grant Calendar, where you can log in to your GrantWatch account today, save a few grants, and explore your pathway to the new era of grant writing with more wins and beyond!

Bringing It Full Circle

Before we close, we need to return to the foundation. In the original book in this series, *The Queen of Grants: From Teacher to Grant Writer to CEO,* I introduced the idea of mapping a grant. Not as a trend. Not as a catchy phrase. But as a discipline. The idea was simple. Every part of a proposal must be connected. The need leads to the goal. The goal leads to measurable objectives. The objectives drive the activities. The activities determine the evaluation. The evaluation supports the budget. When those pieces align, trust is built.

In Chapter 1, *GrantTalk Secrets,* you saw the importance of the mapping principle echoed repeatedly by professionals across the field. Different sectors. Different experiences. Same conclusion. Clarity wins. Structure wins. Alignment wins. That is not a coincidence. It is a pattern for mapping.

This is also where the AI Grant Writing Tool fits in, as discussed in Chapter 4. It is not there to replace your thinking. It is there to organize it. It forces you to slow down and answer the hard questions about your organization, your capacity, your community engagement, and your specific program. It walks you through the same mapped structure we have been discussing from the beginning. It helps you see whether your budget actually reflects your activities. It shows you whether your objectives are measurable or just hopeful statements. It gives you a working draft, but you still bring the depth, the context, and the heart.

Grant writing is not separate from marketing or creating visibility, as discussed in Chapter 2. They are connected. When you clearly define your need, impact, and outcomes, you also clarify your message to donors, partners, and your community. A well-mapped program becomes content for newsletters, social media, presentations, and annual reports. The same clarity that attracts funders also builds credibility and visibility. When your programs are structured and measurable, your story becomes stronger.

I saw this firsthand when my team committed to a 20 Day Platform Challenge as discussed in Chapter 3. We journaled and wrote every single day. We set aside the time. Some days it felt repetitive. Some days it felt messy. We wrote. We rewrote. We refined. We adjusted the message. We paid attention to what resonated and what fell flat. We kept building and rebuilding until the platform became stronger.

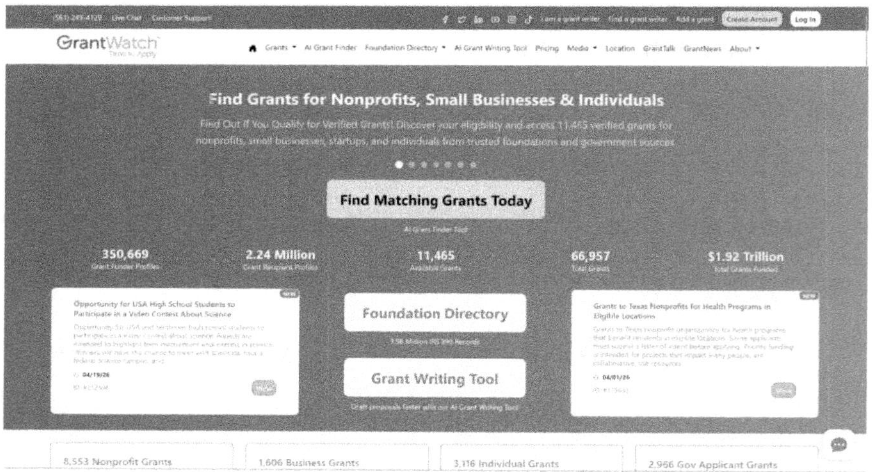

Grant writing works the same way.

You do not draft one proposal and declare yourself finished. You revise. You refine. You learn what funders respond to. You study feedback. You strengthen weak objectives. You tighten evaluation plans. You adjust budgets so they reflect reality. You rebuild programs when something does not work. Even successful proposals can be improved. Even funded programs can be refined.

This is not failure. This is growth.

The new era of grant writing demands organizations that are willing to delve deeper and develop stronger proposals. Expectations are higher. Competition is stronger. Funders want proof, not promises. They want to see that you understand your numbers, your outcomes, and your long-term sustainability. They want to invest in organizations that are visible, consistent, and prepared.

So set aside the time. Treat your grant writing the way we treated the 20 Day Platform Challenge. Show up daily. Map your programs carefully. Rework them until they make sense. Build and rebuild as needed. Strengthen your messaging alongside your structure. Visibility and funding rise together when the foundation is solid.

You have the framework. You have the tools. You have the insight from GrantTalk Secrets. Now go apply it. Refine your grants. Strengthen your programs. Make your impact measurable and visible. Be ready for the new era of grant writing. You got this!

332

ABOUT THE AUTHOR

Libby Hikind, known as the "Queen of Grants," is a wife, mother, grandmother, and great-grandmother, and the Founder and CEO of GrantWatch.com, Libby is also the author of The Queen of Grants: From Teacher to Grant Writer to CEO, the planner of Organizing My Thoughts, Manifesting My Goals, and creator of eight children's books and eight companion coloring books.

With nearly three decades at the NYC Department of Education, Libby launched her first grant writing agency in 1994 and published NYCGrantsWatch, a weekly faxed grant newsletter. In 2010, she built GrantWatch.com, a platform to support nonprofits, businesses, and organizations seeking funding, and GrantWriterTeam in 2012.

Today, GrantWatch is the leading grant-funding search engine serving over 350,000 monthly visitors. Today, the site lists more than 12,000 grants across 61 categories, along with an AI Grant Writing Tool, a Foundation Directory, a Grant Recipient Directory, and a Grants Calendar, and is recognized as number one in the industry.

A frequent media guest and conference speaker, she has appeared on television in DC, Tennessee, New York, and Florida, as well as in virtual TV appearances across the USA.

ACKNOWLEDGMENTS

I want to express my appreciation to all the dedicated individuals at GrantWatch who played key roles in editing this manuscript. A special thank you to my main editors, Susan, Lori, and Ariel, who lived and breathed this book with me. And a thank-you to my husband, Jacob, who gave up his time with me day after day so I could write and rewrite, with the promise of a great vacation for both of us at its conclusion.

I want to thank my advanced readers, Danika, Nikita, and Lianne, for bringing fresh eyes to the proofreading process. I want to thank Pamela for organizing and taking care of our podcast guests.

I'm also grateful to Adrian for helping revise the beautiful book cover originally created by the late Jon Flor, and to The Fellas Media LLC for the outstanding cover photo that keeps me forever young.

I want to thank all the *GrantTalk* guests for their contributions to this book. Your insights have added immense value to this project.

I am truly thankful for Aaron and my staff's collective effort in taking the 20-Day Platform Challenge and for sharing their journaling in this book. I know it wasn't easy to go public with your feelings as we went through this immense transformation, but we learned and grew together.